HEALING THROUGH LOSS AND SELF, DISCOVERY

A Comprehensive Guide to Recovering from Heartbreak, Developing Self, Love, and Achieving Emotional Balance in Life and Relationships

Carina Marvel

© Copyright 2024 by Carina Marvel
Healing Through Loss and Self, Discovery

All rights reserved

Table Of Contents

Introduction _____ 5

Author's preface _____ 7

How to Use This Book _____ 9

Practical Tools and Exercises _____ 12

Chapter 1: The Nature of Love _____ 17

Chapter 2: "The Right Person at the Wrong Time" ___ 28

Chapter 3: "The Wrong Person at the Right Time" ___ 37

Chapter 4: The Impact of Heartbreak _____ 52

Chapter 5: Recognizing Unhealthy Patterns _____ 65

Chapter 6: Acceptance and Closure _____ 94

Chapter 7: Healing a Broken Heart _____ 120

Chapter 8: Forgiveness and Letting Go _____ 135

Chapter 9: Building Self, Esteem _____ 151

Chapter 10: Self, Reflection and Growth _____ 165

Chapter 11: Establishing Healthy Boundaries _____ 175

Chapter 12: Creating Healthy Relationships _____ *192*

Chapter 13: Emotional Balance and Mindfulness _____ *209*

Chapter 14: Moving Forward with Confidence _____ *223*

*Final Words from the Author*_____ *245*

Introduction

In this book, you will discover a true treasure trove of guidance designed to help you heal your heart, cultivate self, love, create harmony in your life and relationships, and stimulate personal growth. Through practical exercises, heartfelt advice, and a variety of effective strategies, this book will support you as you navigate emotional challenges and build a strong sense of self, worth. Drawing from personal experiences and professional insights, it explores key topics such as overcoming emotional pain, boosting self, confidence, nurturing healthy relationships, and achieving balance between work and personal life. You can trust that this book will be a valuable and inspiring resource, helping you make positive changes and guiding you toward emotional stability and self, discovery.

Many of the practices discussed in this book are essential at various stages of personal growth and healing. You might encounter some repetition of techniques in different chapters, and this is intentional, as it reinforces key practices that benefit multiple areas of emotional well, being. By integrating these practices into your daily routine and revisiting them when necessary, you'll find that they become powerful tools to help you face life's challenges more effectively and consistently.

Remember, healing and personal growth are ongoing journeys, and the tools you cultivate along the way are there to support you at every stage of your path.

Author's preface

Dear Reader,

I am incredibly grateful that you've chosen to trust me by picking up this book. It truly means the world to me! As a life coach and through my own personal experiences, I've seen how deeply emotional pain and heartbreak can shake us to our core. I understand how overwhelming, frightening, and disorienting it can feel, but I want you to know that healing and growth aren't just possible. They're within your reach.

This book is a collection of exercises, support, and strategies I've carefully crafted to help you manage your pain and find peace within yourself. My hope is that through these pages, you'll gain the tools and insights needed to boost your self, esteem, build healthy relationships, and create a balanced and fulfilling life. Yes, there will be challenging moments, but with the right mindset and a bit of faith, I firmly believe that anything is possible.

Consider this book your trusted companion, filled with evidence, based insights and practical advice. Each chapter is designed to address the specific challenges you might face, whether it's overcoming pain and fear or managing stress and anxiety. My ultimate goal is to help you shape a life brimming with happiness, love, and emotional well, being.

Remember, change is possible. Just by opening this book, you've already taken the first step toward a brighter and more fulfilling future. I'm excited to share this journey with you.

With all my love and appreciation,
Carina Marvel

How to Use This Book

Before diving into the content, let's take a moment to understand how to get the most out of this book:

1. **Set Your Intention**: Take a moment to reflect on why you picked up this book. What are your goals and aspirations? Are you looking to heal from heartbreak, build self, esteem, create healthy relationships, or find balance in your life? Setting a clear intention will help you focus your energy and make the most of the journey ahead.

2. **Be Open and Willing**: Healing and personal growth require openness and a willingness to explore new perspectives and try different techniques. Approach the content with an open mind and be ready to challenge some of your beliefs and habits.

3. **Engage in Self, Reflection**: Throughout the book, you'll find exercises and reflection prompts. Take the time to engage in these activities and journal your thoughts. This will deepen your understanding and help you apply the concepts to your daily life.

4. **Take It at Your Own Pace**: Healing and growth are personal journeys, and everyone progresses at their own speed. There's no rush or pressure to finish the book quickly. Take your time, absorb the material, and integrate it into your life at a pace that feels comfortable to you.

5. **Apply What Resonates**: Not every concept or technique may resonate with you, and that's okay. Take what feels right for you and leave the rest. Trust your instincts and apply the strategies that align with your values and goals.

6. **Seek Support**: Remember, you don't have to go through this journey alone. Reach out to trusted friends, family members, or professionals for support. Connecting with others who are on a similar path can provide additional insights and encouragement.

7. **Embrace Imperfection**: Healing and growth are not linear processes. There will be ups and downs, setbacks, and breakthroughs. Embrace the imperfections and be kind to yourself. Remember that progress, no matter how small, is still progress.

Now that you have an idea of how to approach this book, let's embark on this transformative journey together. Get ready to discover the power within you to heal, grow, and create a life filled with love, joy, and emotional balance.

Practical Tools and Exercises

Building emotional resilience requires practical tools and exercises that can be seamlessly integrated into your daily life, even if it's just for a few minutes each day, but with consistency. These activities are ideal for supporting your healing process and helping you develop a stronger, more grounded sense of self. Remember, healing is a journey that demands time, effort, and consistency.

Below are some powerful tools and exercises to support you along the way:

Journaling

Writing down your thoughts, sensations, and feelings can be a cathartic and transformative experience. Set aside time each day to reflect on your emotions and experiences. Use your journal as a safe space to express yourself without judgment, exploring your fears, hopes, and dreams. This practice helps you gain clarity, better process your emotions, and track your progress over time. Write down what you're feeling, even when it seems hard to put into words, because looking back on what you've written over time will give you the awareness of how much you've grown.

Self, Compassion Meditation

Practicing self, compassion is essential for healing. For 10, 15 minutes, find a quiet place, sit comfortably, close your eyes, and take three deep breaths, then continue breathing normally. Repeat positive affirmations like "I deserve love and happiness" or "I deserve healing," choosing the one that resonates most with you. Visualize love and compassion wrapping around your body, embracing your pain with kindness and understanding. This practice helps build a deeper connection with yourself, offering relief from negative emotions.

Gratitude Practice

Cultivating gratitude can transform your perspective and bring more positivity into your life. Each day, write down three things you're grateful for. These can be simple things like a beautiful sunset, a friend's kind gesture, or a delicious meal, but also think about deeper aspects like your health, your home, or small personal achievements. Gratitude helps shift focus toward the positives in life, even during tough times, and directs attention away from problems and toward blessings. Just 10, 15 minutes a day, either in the morning or before bed, can make a significant impact on your mood and how you approach the day.

Visualization

Visualization is an incredibly powerful tool for manifesting your desires and goals. Close your eyes and imagine yourself healed and thriving. Picture the life you want to create, the loving relationships you desire, and the emotional balance you seek. Engage all your senses and feel the emotions associated with this vision. When practiced daily, this technique can help align your thoughts, beliefs, and actions with the reality you want to achieve. I recommend doing this after practicing gratitude for at least 10 minutes, but feel free to extend it as long as you like.

Self, Care Rituals

Self, care is crucial for nurturing your emotional well, being. Create a self, care routine that includes activities you enjoy and that make you feel good. It could be taking a relaxing bath, going for a walk in nature, practicing yoga, or reading a book. Choose activities that nurture your mind, body, and spirit, and that bring you back to yourself when you feel lost or overwhelmed. Prioritize self, care and make it a non, negotiable part of your daily life.

Affirmations

Affirmations are positive statements that can reprogram your subconscious mind and boost your self, esteem. You can say them out loud (especially when you're alone), whisper them, or even think them. If you prefer, you can record them and listen to them repeatedly, the more often you repeat them, the more effective they become! Choose affirmations that resonate with you, such as "I am loved," "I am a winner," or "I deserve love and happiness." Affirmations help you reframe negative beliefs and build a positive mindset. Remember that, like any practice, consistency is key.

Support Network

Building a support network is essential during the healing process. Surround yourself with people who uplift and support you. Seek out friends, family members, or support groups who can provide a listening ear and offer guidance. Connecting with others who have experienced similar challenges can be incredibly healing and reassuring. Don't hesitate to reach out when you need help, as true courage lies in admitting that you can't do everything on your own.

Remember, these tools and exercises can be adapted to your unique needs and preferences. Experiment with different practices and find what resonates with you. Be patient with yourself and celebrate every small step forward on your journey to healing and self, discovery.

Chapter 1:
The Nature of Love

Love is perhaps the most complex and beautiful emotion that we, as humans, are privileged to experience. It has the profound power to uplift us, bring joy to our lives, and remind us of what truly matters. At its best, love can fill our lives with meaning and a sense of belonging. But as much as love can enrich us, it can also bring about pain, suffering, and confusion.

In this chapter, we will explore the multifaceted nature of love. Love does not adhere to a universal mold, each one of us experiences and idealizes it differently. Whether it manifests as romantic love, familial love, or platonic love, every form has its own unique dynamics. Romantic love, for instance, may involve passion, desire, and intimacy, while familial love is often characterized by unconditional support and care.

It's vital to recognize that love is not always easy. Relationships can be challenging, and conflicts are often inevitable. But it is through these moments of difficulty that we have the opportunity to grow, both individually and together with our partners. Love invites us into self, discovery, showing us what we need, desire, and where our boundaries lie. It reveals our strengths as well as our vulnerabilities. Through love, we also learn to communicate, navigate complex emotions, and develop a deeper sense of empathy for others.

At times, love can be a source of deep pain. The experience of loss, rejection, or betrayal can leave us feeling shattered, confused, and questioning our self, worth. However, it's important to remember that suffering in love does not signal the end of the road, it presents an opportunity for growth. Just as we endured many painful falls before learning to walk as children, the challenges in love teach us resilience and open the door to healthier, more fulfilling relationships in the future.

In this chapter, we'll dive into the complexities, challenges, and transformative power of love. By understanding its nature and nurturing our emotional well, being, we can foster meaningful connections that bring happiness and fulfillment into our lives. Love is, after all, one of the most powerful forces within us, capable of profound transformation when understood and embraced with care.

What Is Love?

Love is a complex and multifaceted emotion that has intrigued poets, philosophers, and scientists for centuries. It is a force that permeates every part of our lives, shaping our relationships, self, perception, and overall well, being. In this chapter, we will explore the many dimensions of love and gain a deeper understanding of how profoundly it impacts our lives.

Love is an intrinsic part of the human experience, transcending cultural, geographical, and temporal boundaries. It connects us to others and brings meaning to our existence. From the love we receive as children to the love we seek throughout our lives, it is a driving force that shapes our emotional landscape.

But love isn't just about romantic relationships. It extends to our families, friends, and even the love we develop for ourselves. Each form of love carries its own joys, challenges, and lessons.

Love manifests in many ways, each with its unique qualities and dynamics. Let's take a look at some of the most common types:

- **Platonic Love** is a powerful force often overlooked. The connection between friends, built on respect, trust, and shared experiences, can be as fulfilling and meaningful as romantic love. It is a bond that can last a lifetime, bringing comfort and joy, especially in times of need.

- **Romantic Love** is often seen as the pinnacle of love, filled with passion and intensity. This type of love can be exhilarating, but it also demands effort and communication to keep it thriving.

- **Familial Love** is the deep bond we share with family, providing us with a sense of security and belonging. It is the foundation that often shapes our emotional well, being from an early age.

- **Self, Love** is perhaps the most important form of love. Accepting ourselves, setting boundaries, and practicing self, care are essential for leading an authentic and fulfilling life. Cultivating self, love is not only crucial for our well, being but also vital to the health of all our relationships.

Love, in all its forms, is a transformative and powerful force. Love has the capacity to change our lives in remarkable ways. It can heal emotional wounds, inspire personal growth, and foster a sense of connection and belonging. It brings joy, meaning, and purpose. However, it's important to recognize that love can also bring pain and suffering, and at times, it can even become toxic. The vulnerability that comes with love can leave us open to hurt and disappointment.

Understanding the complexities of love is essential for navigating its ups and downs. When we feel loved and supported, we experience a sense of security and happiness. Research has shown that love offers countless benefits for our mental and physical health, such as reducing stress, increasing resilience, and improving life satisfaction.

That said, relying solely on external sources for love can be detrimental. Cultivating self, love and self, compassion are essential for maintaining emotional balance and building healthy relationships.

Love is not a destination but a journey, one of growth, learning, and self, discovery. Throughout our lives, we will experience different forms of love and navigate their complexities. Embracing this journey requires openness, vulnerability, and a willingness to evolve.

As we continue through this book, we'll explore love in all its intricacies. We'll uncover how love shapes our lives, influences our choices, and impacts our well, being. Together, we'll embark on a transformative journey of healing, self, discovery, and emotional balance.

The Role of Self, Love in Relationships

Self, love is a fundamental aspect of building healthy and fulfilling relationships. When we love ourselves, we are better able to love and connect with others. In this chapter, we will explore the role of self, love in relationships and how it can contribute to emotional balance and personal growth.

- **The Foundation of Self, Love** Self, love is not a destination but a lifelong journey. It begins with accepting ourselves as we are, embracing our strengths and weaknesses, and recognizing our inherent worth. When we cultivate self, love, we develop a deep sense of compassion and kindness towards ourselves, which becomes the foundation for nurturing healthy relationships.
  Important: Self, love involves setting healthy boundaries, practicing self, care, and prioritizing our needs and well, being.

- **Authenticity in Relationships** When we love ourselves, we are more likely to show up authentically in our relationships. Authenticity means being true to ourselves, expressing our thoughts and emotions honestly, and allowing others to do the same. By embracing our authentic selves, we create space for genuine connections and open communication.

- *Important:* Authenticity requires vulnerability and the willingness to be seen and accepted for who we truly are.

- **Emotional Availability** Self, love enables us to be emotionally available to our partners. When we prioritize our emotional well, being, we are better able to understand and regulate our own emotions, which allows us to be present and supportive in our relationships. Emotional availability fosters trust, intimacy, and deeper connections.

- *Important:* Emotional availability involves active listening, empathy, and validating our partner's emotions.

- **Respect and Boundaries** In healthy relationships, respect and boundaries are essential. When we love ourselves, we recognize our own worth and value, and we expect to be treated with respect. Setting and maintaining boundaries is crucial for preserving our emotional well, being and ensuring that our needs are met.

- *Important:* Respect and boundaries are a two, way street, requiring open communication and mutual understanding.

- **Conflict Resolution** Self, love plays a significant role in conflict resolution within relationships. When we love ourselves, we approach conflicts with compassion and a desire for resolution. We are better able to manage our emotions, communicate effectively, and find mutually beneficial solutions.
  Important: Conflict resolution requires active listening, empathy, and a willingness to find common ground.

- **Growth and Support** In relationships where self, love is nurtured, both partners have the opportunity for personal growth and support. When we love ourselves, we encourage our partners to pursue their dreams and goals, celebrate their successes, and provide a safe space for them to share their vulnerabilities.
  Important: Supporting our partners' growth requires trust, encouragement, and a belief in their potential.

Self, love is not selfish; it is a necessary ingredient for building healthy and fulfilling relationships. When we prioritize our own well, being and cultivate self, love, we create a solid foundation for emotional balance, personal growth, and meaningful connections with others.

Important: Remember, self, love is a journey, and it requires ongoing commitment and practice. Embrace the process, be patient with yourself, and celebrate the progress you make along the way.

Poem: In the Heart of a Lover

Oh love, you mysterious muse,

A force that sweeps us away, leaves us bruised.

In the deepest corners of our hearts, you bloom,

Bringing both joy and sorrow, light and gloom.

With every heartbeat, love's rhythm plays,

A symphony of emotions in endless ways.

It lifts us high on wings of delight,

Only to plunge us into the dark of night.

What lies in the heart of a lover, you ask?

A tapestry of dreams, hidden beneath life's mask.

A longing for connection, raw and pure,

To find comfort in arms that hold us secure.

To be seen, cherished, flaws and all,

And caught by love when we start to fall.

Love is a journey, a path untamed,

Where feelings collide and cannot be named.

Amidst the pain, a strength is born,

A resilience that shines like the morning dawn.

For love's lessons, though sometimes harsh,

Can lead us to a self reborn from the ash.

So, dear soul, as you walk love's road,

Know that healing and growth are a shared load.

Embrace the highs, the lows, the tears,

For within them, your true self appears.

In the heart of a lover, a fire does burn,

A longing to grow, to love, to learn.

To find peace, self, love, and harmony,

And unlock the door to emotional mastery.

Let your heart be your guide,

As you journey through love, let it be your stride.

Through loss and self, discovery, you'll find,

A love that's enduring, gentle, and kind.

Chapter 2:
"The Right Person at the Wrong Time"

Now we delve into a complex topic that resonates deeply with my personal experiences: meeting the "right person at the wrong time." This chapter explores the bittersweet experience of encountering a potential partner when external circumstances or personal growth hinder the development of a relationship.

We begin by acknowledging the universal desire for love and connection, highlighting the excitement that arises when meeting someone who seems to be the perfect match. However, we also emphasize the importance of timing in relationships and the impact it can have on their outcome.

Timing is Everything

The concept of timing is explored in, depth, recognizing that individuals evolve and change over time. It is crucial to acknowledge that personal growth and life circumstances can influence the success or failure of a relationship. By understanding this reality, we can gain a sense of acceptance and perspective, ultimately facilitating our healing process.

Developing Self, Awareness

Developing self, awareness is key when navigating the scenario of meeting the right person (with whom we feel deeply connected) at the wrong time. Reflecting on our own emotional needs, desires, and goals can help us gain clarity on whether pursuing a relationship at a particular time is truly in our best interest. Self, awareness empowers us to make informed decisions and prioritize our emotional well, being.

Open and Honest Communication

Open and honest communication is essential when dealing with the right person at the wrong time. This chapter emphasizes the importance of setting clear boundaries and expressing our needs and limitations. By openly discussing expectations and concerns, individuals can establish a foundation of trust and understanding, even if the relationship cannot progress at the moment.

Embracing Personal Growth

This chapter encourages embracing personal growth and self, discovery during this challenging time. By focusing on our own development and pursuing our passions and goals, we can find solace and fulfillment outside of a romantic relationship.

Letting Go with Love

Finally, the chapter addresses the difficult but necessary step of letting go when the timing is not right. It explores the concept of letting go with love, emphasizing that releasing a potential partner does not diminish the connection or the value of the experience. This section offers strategies and insights for finding closure and moving forward with grace and self, compassion.

Recognizing When Timing Is Off

As we know, timing plays a crucial role in various aspects of our lives, including relationships, career opportunities, and personal growth. Often, it seems like life throws challenges at us, making us doubt whether the moment is right for certain decisions or actions.

By understanding the signs and learning to trust our intuition, we can make informed choices that align with our values and aspirations.

When it comes to relationships, it is essential to be attentive to the signs that the timing might not be right. These signs can manifest in various ways:

Conflicting Priorities

When you and your partner have different goals or priorities that do not align, it might be a sign that the timing is off. It is crucial to have open and honest conversations to understand each other's needs and aspirations.

Lack of Emotional Availability

If either you or your partner is not emotionally available or ready for a committed and reciprocal relationship, it might indicate that the timing is not ideal. It is vital to be honest with yourself and your partner about your emotional state.

External Pressures

Sometimes, external factors such as work, family, or personal circumstances can create obstacles that make it difficult for a relationship to thrive. Recognizing these pressures can help you evaluate whether the timing is right and potentially find ways to address them.

Similarly, in other areas of life, such as career and personal growth, there are signs that the timing might not be optimal:

Feeling Stuck

If you feel stagnant or dissatisfied in your career or personal aspirations, it might indicate that the timing is off. It is essential to reflect on your goals and aspirations and consider whether it is time for a change.

Overwhelm and Burnout

When you constantly feel overwhelmed and exhausted, it might be a sign that you are pushing yourself too hard or taking on too much. Recognizing these factors can help you prioritize self, care and find a healthier and more constructive balance.

Resistance and Lack of Flow

If you constantly encounter resistance or obstacles in your efforts, it might be a sign that the timing is not aligned. Pay attention to the level of ease and flow in your activities.

Trusting Your Intuition

Recognizing when the timing is off requires tuning into your intuition and listening to your inner voice. Listening to yourself is always fundamental. Intuition is a powerful tool we all possess that can guide us toward decisions aligned with our highest good.

Here are some steps to help you trust your intuition:

- **Cultivate Mindfulness:** Practice mindfulness to develop a deeper connection with your inner self. Take time to quiet your mind, listen to your thoughts and feelings, and become aware of the subtle messages your intuition may be sending.

- **Pay Attention to Your Body:** Your body often provides valuable clues about whether the timing is right or wrong. Notice any physical sensations or discomfort that arise when you think about a particular decision or action.

- **Journaling:** Writing in a journal can help you gain clarity and tap into your intuition. Dedicate regular time to writing and let your thoughts and feelings flow onto the paper without judgment.

- **Seek Support:** Discuss your thoughts and concerns with a trusted friend, mentor, or therapist. Sometimes, an outside perspective can provide valuable insights and help you gain clarity.

Navigating When Timing Is Off

Once you recognize that the timing is off, it is important to navigate these situations with grace and wisdom. Here are some strategies to help you when the timing is not right:

- **Practice Patience:** Accept that sometimes things take time and that the universe has its own timing. Cultivate patience and trust that the right opportunities will come at the right moment. It's a powerful tool!

- **Focus on Personal Development:** Use the time to invest in your personal growth and self, care. Explore new hobbies, learn new skills, or engage in activities that bring you joy and fulfillment.

- **Reevaluate Your Goals:** Take the opportunity to reassess your goals and aspirations. Are they still aligned with your values and desires? Use this time to realign your goals with your current circumstances and aspirations.

- **Practice Gratitude:** Cultivate a mindset of gratitude and focus on the blessings in your life. Gratitude can help you shift your perspective and bring a sense of peace and fulfillment, even when the timing is not ideal. Remember, even if the current moment doesn't seem perfect, we always have much to be grateful for!

Recognizing when the timing is off is a valuable skill that can lead to greater self, awareness and emotional well, being. Trust your intuition, navigate with grace, and have faith that the right timing will align with your highest good.

Chapter 3:
"The Wrong Person at the Right Time"

There are moments in life when we find ourselves in relationships that seem ideal on the surface, yet something deep within tells us that not everything is as it seems. It's like wearing a smiling mask while feeling an undercurrent of unease or dissatisfaction. Often, we convince ourselves that this relationship is what we need at that moment, even though, in reality, we might just be trying to fill a void or find stability during chaotic times. We settle because the fear of being alone or facing the unknown pushes us to stay, despite knowing that this person isn't truly our match.

The idea of leaving such a relationship can seem insurmountable, but recognizing this feeling is the first step toward healing. It's important to understand that we deserve more than just the appearance of happiness. Only when we have the courage to face these truths can we free ourselves from the burden of settling and open up to the possibility of finding authentic and fulfilling love. It's crucial to recognize that being with the "wrong person at the right time" is not a failure or a reflection of our worth, but a common experience that many of us go through, and it represents an opportunity for growth and self, discovery.

The Illusion of Perfection

When we meet someone who seems to check all the boxes and makes us feel alive, it's easy to get swept away by the excitement and the promise of a fairy tale romance. We might ignore red flags or dismiss our intuition because we're so captivated by the idea of being with someone who seems perfect.

However, perfection is an illusion. No one is perfect, and relationships require effort and compromise from both sides. It's important to remember that a healthy relationship is built on mutual respect, trust, and open communication.

Our intuition is a powerful tool that can guide us toward what is right for us. However, when we're infatuated with someone, we might ignore our intuition or brush off any doubts that arise. We might convince ourselves that we're overthinking or being too cautious.

But our intuition is there to protect us and guide us toward what's best for our emotional well, being and beyond. If something feels off or if we have recurring doubts, it's important to listen to our intuition and explore those feelings further.

The Importance of Self, Reflection

These experiences can be opportunities for self, reflection and growth. They are chances to examine our patterns and beliefs, and to understand what we truly want and need in a relationship.

Take time to reflect on your past relationships and ask yourself what patterns you've noticed, what emotions you've felt, and why. Are there specific traits or behaviors that you're consistently drawn to? Are there unresolved issues from the past that may be influencing your choices?

Learning to Trust Yourself

Trusting yourself and your intuition is a fundamental part of cultivating healthy relationships. When we're with the "wrong person at the right time, " we may doubt our judgment and question our ability to make good choices.

But it's important to remember that we have the power to make decisions that align with our values and needs. Trust yourself and your intuition. Trust that you have the strength and wisdom to choose what's best for you.

Letting Go and Growing

Recognizing that you're with the wrong person at the right time requires courage, but it's an essential step for growth and moving forward. Remember, you deserve a relationship that makes you feel loved and valued for who you truly are. Letting go of what no longer serves you will make room for new opportunities and genuine connections.

Every experience, even the difficult ones, has the potential to teach us something valuable about ourselves and what we truly desire. Use this time to reflect, grow, and prepare yourself for the kind of love you truly deserve.

Continue believing in yourself and your journey, knowing that each decision you make in alignment with your well, being brings you closer to the life and relationships you dream of.

Facing Relationships with Unfit Partners

When it comes to relationships, we all hope to find love, support, and a deep connection with our partner. However, sometimes we end up in relationships with individuals who aren't right for us. These relationships can be emotionally draining and even toxic, impacting our mental and emotional well, being. In this section, we'll explore how to identify and manage relationships with unfit partners, and, ultimately, find the strength to let go and move forward with self, assurance.

Recognizing the Signs

It's crucial to recognize the early signs of an unfit partner. These may include:

- **Emotional Unavailability**: Your partner may be distant, unwilling, or unable to share their emotions and connect on a deeper level.

- **Lack of Respect and Support**: Disregarding your feelings, dismissing your opinions, or failing to support your aspirations can indicate a lack of respect.

- **Constant Criticism and Belittling**: If your partner frequently puts you down or makes you feel unworthy, this is a clear red flag.

- **Manipulative or Controlling Behavior**: Attempts to control your actions, isolate you from loved ones, or manipulate your emotions are signs of a toxic dynamic.

- **Inability to Communicate Effectively**: Communication is key in any relationship. If your partner is unwilling or unable to communicate openly and honestly, it can lead to unresolved conflicts and misunderstandings.

Trust your instincts and pay attention to your emotional responses in the relationship. If you often feel drained, anxious, or unhappy, it may be a sign that your partner is not right for you.

Setting Boundaries

After recognizing that you are in a relationship with an unfit partner, setting boundaries becomes crucial. Boundaries are necessary to protect your emotional well, being and to establish clear expectations for how you deserve to be treated. Communicate these boundaries to your partner and be firm in enforcing them. Remember, boundaries are about taking care of yourself, not about controlling the other person.

Seeking Support

Dealing with a relationship involving an unfit partner can be emotionally challenging and overwhelming. Reach out to friends, family, or a therapist for support. Surrounding yourself with people who care about you can provide the guidance and encouragement needed to make difficult decisions. A support system offers a safe space to express your feelings and gain perspective on the situation.

Letting Go and Moving Forward

Ending a relationship with an unfit partner can be one of the hardest decisions you'll ever make, but it's often necessary for your emotional and mental well, being. Letting go requires immense strength and self, love. Always remember that you deserve to be in a relationship that is healthy, supportive, and loving.

Here are some steps to help you move forward:

- **Acceptance**: Accept that the relationship is not serving you and that it's okay to prioritize your well, being.

- **Self, Compassion**: Be gentle with yourself as you go through the process of letting go. It's normal to feel a mix of emotions, from sadness to relief.

- **Focus on Self, Growth**: Use this time to focus on your personal growth and self, care. Reconnect with activities and hobbies that bring you joy and fulfillment.

- **Build a Support System**: Surround yourself with people who uplift and support you. Share your experiences and lean on your loved ones for guidance and encouragement.

- **Trust the Process**: Healing is not linear. Trust that, in time, you will find peace and clarity, and be open to the possibility of healthier, more fulfilling relationships in the future.

By letting go of relationships that no longer serve you, you make room for self, discovery, healing, and the opportunity to find a partnership that truly aligns with your values and desires. Stay strong, trust yourself, and remember that you are worthy of love and happiness.

Understanding Our Emotional Choices

To heal and grow from emotional pain, it's crucial to understand the choices we make in our emotional lives. Our emotions influence our thoughts, actions, and overall well, being significantly. By gaining insight into these emotional choices, we can make more conscious decisions that guide us toward healing and personal growth.

The Power of Awareness

Developing self, awareness is the first step in understanding our emotional choices. This involves observing our thoughts, feelings, and behaviors without judgment. By becoming aware of our emotional patterns and triggers, we can identify any unhealthy or self, destructive behaviors that may be hindering our growth. This awareness allows us to recognize when we're falling into old patterns and gives us the opportunity to choose a different, more positive response.

Recognizing Emotional Triggers

Emotional triggers are events, situations, or even people that provoke strong emotional reactions within us. These reactions often stem from past experiences and can evoke feelings like anger, sadness, or fear. By identifying and understanding our triggers, we can begin to distinguish between past wounds and present experiences, helping us respond more consciously rather than reacting impulsively.

The Role of Beliefs and Values

Our beliefs and values shape how we see the world and influence the choices we make. It's essential to examine these beliefs and values to ensure they align with our goals for emotional healing and growth. Limiting beliefs can create negative narratives that trap us in unproductive emotional cycles. Reframing these beliefs empowers us to make healthier choices that support our well, being.

Emotional Intelligence

Emotional intelligence is our ability to recognize, understand, and manage our own emotions and those of others. Developing emotional intelligence helps us navigate our emotions with greater ease and make more informed decisions. This includes building skills such as self, regulation, empathy, and effective communication. By increasing our emotional intelligence, we can improve our relationships and manage stress more effectively.

Cultivating Mindfulness

Mindfulness is the practice of being fully present and engaged in the current moment. It involves observing our thoughts and emotions without judgment, which fosters greater self, awareness. By practicing mindfulness, we can respond to our emotions with intention and compassion rather than reacting out of habit or impulse. This helps create a calmer and more balanced emotional state.

The Power of Choice

Understanding our emotional choices gives us the power to take responsibility for our emotional well, being. We can choose how we respond to our emotions and the situations that arise in our lives. By making conscious choices aligned with our values and goals, we can pave a path toward self, love and emotional balance.

Moving Forward

Remember, you have the power to decide how you navigate your emotional journey. Each choice you make is an opportunity to heal, grow, and evolve in every aspect of your life. Embrace this power with kindness and compassion, knowing that every step forward, no matter how small, brings you closer to a more balanced and fulfilling life.

Poem: The Right Love at the Wrong Time

She was a tempest, emotions swirling wild,

Her heart yearning for love, deep and untamed.

He appeared in her life like a dazzling star,

A love so radiant, it left her forever changed.

Their timing was cruel, paths not meant to cross,

And their love, so fervent, began to unravel.

They danced in the moonlight, hearts intertwined,

But reality broke the dreams they had traveled.

She clung to the hope of what might have been,

But deep down she knew, a new journey must begin.

A path of healing, of finding her worth,

To rise from the ashes, to reclaim her rebirth.

For the wrong love at the right time has its own gifts,

Lessons of resilience, and growth in the rifts.

She learned to release, to embrace the ache,

And to find the dawn after the heartache.

Though scars remain, etched deep in her soul,

She emerged with a strength that made her whole.

For the wrong love at the right time was a flame,

A spark that ignited her soul's true name.

She discovered herself, her voice, her light,

And vowed to love herself with all her might.

So to those who've loved and lost along the way,

Remember, wrong love clears the path for a brighter day.

Chapter 4:
The Impact of Heartbreak

Heartbreak is a universal experience that can leave us feeling shattered and lost. It has the power to turn our lives upside down, making us question our self, worth and our capacity to give and receive love. While the pain of heartbreak can be overwhelming, it's important to remember that it is a natural part of the human experience. In this chapter, we'll delve into the profound impact of heartbreak and how it shapes our lives.

Heartbreak isn't just an emotional experience; it also has tangible physical and psychological effects. When we go through it, our body responds with stress, releasing hormones like cortisol and adrenaline, which can lead to physical symptoms such as headaches, stomachaches, and fatigue. Our immune system may also weaken, making us more vulnerable to illness. Psychologically, heartbreak can stir feelings of sadness, anger, and confusion, affecting our self, esteem and our ability to trust others.

However, heartbreak doesn't mark the end of the story. In fact, it can serve as a powerful catalyst for personal growth and self, discovery. This painful experience forces us to confront our deepest fears and insecurities, providing us with the opportunity to reflect on past relationships and learn from our mistakes. Through this pain, we gain a deeper understanding of ourselves and what we truly want and need in a relationship.

A crucial aspect of healing from heartbreak is allowing ourselves to grieve. Grief is a natural response to loss, and it's vital to give ourselves permission to feel the accompanying pain and sadness. Healing is not a linear process, and there's no set timeline for moving on. Everyone's healing journey is unique, and it's important to respect your own process.

During this time, practicing self, care and self, compassion is essential. This means taking time to nurture yourself physically, emotionally, and spiritually. Engaging in activities that bring you joy and comfort can help soothe your pain and provide solace. It's also important to surround yourself with supportive friends and loved ones who can offer a listening ear and emotional support.

While heartbreak can be devastating, it also presents an opportunity for growth and self, discovery. Through the healing process, we can learn to love ourselves more deeply and develop a stronger sense of self, worth. We can clarify what we truly desire and need in a relationship, and we can cultivate healthier patterns of communication and behavior. Healing from heartbreak isn't easy, but with time, patience, and self, compassion, it's possible to rediscover joy and fulfillment.

Emotional and Physical Effects

Heartbreak is an intense and deeply personal experience that can significantly impact both our emotional and physical well, being. The end of a significant relationship or a deep emotional connection can leave us feeling disoriented, overwhelmed, and, at times, physically unwell. Understanding these effects is crucial for navigating the healing process, allowing us to approach our emotions and physical symptoms with greater awareness and care.

Emotional Effects

- **Intense Sadness and Grief:** Heartbreak often brings a wave of overwhelming sadness and grief, similar to mourning a profound loss. This sadness isn't just about missing the other person but also involves the dreams and future plans tied to that relationship. The grief can resemble the mourning process experienced when losing a loved one, including stages such as denial, anger, bargaining, depression, and acceptance. Unlike other forms of loss, heartbreak can involve a complex mix of emotions, such as guilt and regret, making it particularly challenging to process.

- **Loss of Self, Worth:** The end of a relationship can severely impact self, esteem, leading to questions like, "Was I not enough?" or "What did I do wrong?" These doubts can foster a negative self, image and diminish self, worth. This emotional turmoil is often compounded by societal and cultural expectations that measure personal success through relationships. The inner critic becomes louder, and negative self, talk can create a downward spiral of self, blame and feelings of inadequacy.

- **Loneliness and Isolation:** Heartbreak often leads to profound loneliness, especially if the relationship was a central part of your life. The absence of a significant other creates a void, leading to feelings of isolation, even when surrounded by others. This loneliness is not only about missing the person's presence but also about losing the emotional support and companionship they provided. The sudden change in daily routines and the absence of someone to share life's moments with can amplify these feelings.

- **Anxiety and Fear:** The uncertainty accompanying the end of a relationship can trigger anxiety and fear about the future. Concerns about being alone, the possibility of not finding love again, and the fear of being vulnerable in future relationships can create a heightened state of anxiety. This anxiety can manifest as obsessive thoughts, difficulty concentrating, and a constant feeling of unease. The mind often spirals into worst, case scenarios, feeding the anxiety cycle and making it difficult to focus on the present.

- **Depression and Hopelessness:** In some cases, the emotional aftermath of heartbreak can lead to symptoms of depression, including a persistent feeling of hopelessness, loss of interest in activities previously enjoyed, changes in appetite, and sleep disturbances. This despair can feel overwhelming, making it difficult to see a way forward. Depression can also intensify feelings of loneliness and isolation, creating a cycle that is hard to break without support.

Physical Effects

- **Loss of Appetite or Overeating:** Emotional distress from heartbreak can significantly impact eating habits. Some people may lose their appetite entirely, finding it difficult to eat due to a constant feeling of nausea or tightness in the chest. Others might turn to food for comfort, leading to overeating and potential weight gain. The relationship between emotions and eating is complex, and during stressful times, it's common for eating patterns to become disrupted.

- **Sleep Disturbances:** Heartbreak can wreak havoc on sleep. The mind's constant rehashing of the relationship, coupled with anxiety about the future, can make it difficult to fall asleep or stay asleep. This can lead to insomnia or, conversely, an excessive desire to sleep as a means of escaping emotional pain. The lack of restful sleep further exacerbates emotional distress, creating a vicious cycle that can be hard to break.

- **Physical Pain and Fatigue:** The emotional toll of heartbreak often manifests physically, with symptoms such as headaches, muscle tension, chest pain, and a general sense of fatigue. This phenomenon, sometimes referred to as "broken heart syndrome," is a real condition where emotional stress leads to physical heart symptoms similar to those of a heart attack. The body responds to emotional pain by releasing stress hormones like cortisol, which can cause or exacerbate physical pain.

- **Compromised Immune System:** Prolonged emotional stress, such as that experienced during heartbreak, can weaken the immune system, making the body more susceptible to illnesses. This is because the body's stress response diverts energy away from the immune system towards more immediate survival functions, leaving us vulnerable to colds, infections, and other ailments.

Understanding these emotional and physical effects is the first crucial step toward healing. It's important to recognize that these symptoms are normal responses to emotional pain and that seeking support is a vital part of the journey. As we explore recovery strategies in the following chapters, remember that this journey is not a linear process, and it is essential to be patient and compassionate with yourself during this time. Engaging in self, care practices, surrounding yourself with positive and supportive people, and giving yourself time to process everything are all vital steps for moving forward.

The Stages of Grief in Breakups

Navigating the emotional journey of a breakup is rarely straightforward. Healing is not a simple, linear process, and the stages of grief in breakups can differ greatly from person to person, even though they tend to follow a familiar pattern. By understanding and acknowledging these stages, you can better manage your own healing process.

Shock and Denial

When a relationship ends, it's common to initially experience shock and denial. This stage often involves a sense of disbelief and an unwillingness to accept the reality of the breakup. You might find yourself clinging to the hope that the relationship can still be salvaged or that your ex will change their mind. This stage serves as a natural defense mechanism, helping to shield you from the intense emotions that accompany the loss. It's important to allow yourself to feel these emotions and give yourself time to come to terms with what has happened.

Anger and Resentment

As the shock begins to fade, you may start to feel anger and resentment toward your ex, partner. This stage is characterized by feelings of betrayal, injustice, and frustration. It's essential to remember that these emotions are a normal part of the healing process. While it's understandable to feel anger, it's also important to find healthy ways to express these emotions. Activities like journaling, exercising, or speaking with a trusted friend or therapist can help you process and release these feelings constructively.

Bargaining

In the bargaining stage, you might find yourself wishing you could go back and change things. You may even make promises to yourself or your ex, partner in an effort to rekindle the relationship. This stage often reflects a desire to regain a sense of control over the situation. While it's natural to want to fix things, it's important to focus on your own growth and healing during this time.

Depression

As the reality of the breakup settles in, feelings of deep sadness, loneliness, and despair may emerge. This stage is often marked by a profound sense of loss and grief. It's important to give yourself permission to mourn the end of the relationship and to process these emotions. During this stage, practicing self, care and seeking support from loved ones is crucial. Engaging in activities that bring you joy and comfort can help alleviate some of the depression's symptoms.

Acceptance

The final stage of grief in a breakup is acceptance. This stage is characterized by a sense of peace and an understanding that the relationship has ended. Acceptance doesn't necessarily mean you're happy about the breakup, but rather that you've come to terms with it. During this stage, focusing on personal growth and self, discovery is important. Reflect on the lessons learned from the relationship and use them as stepping stones toward a brighter future.

Remember, healing from a breakup takes time and patience. Be gentle with yourself and allow yourself to experience the full range of emotions that come with the grieving process. By recognizing and understanding these stages, you can navigate your healing journey with greater clarity and compassion.

Essay: "When Love Ends"

When love ends, it feels like the ground beneath us has shifted, leaving us unsteady and unsure of where to step next. The pain that follows is a unique kind of suffering, intertwining with our very being and challenging our understanding of ourselves and our place in the world. It is a profound loss, not just of the loved one, but of the future we had envisioned with them, the shared dreams, and the identity we had built in their presence.

The end of love is often accompanied by a whirlwind of emotions, grief, anger, confusion, and deep sadness. These feelings can be overwhelming, making it hard to see beyond the immediate hurt. Yet, within this turmoil lies an opportunity for transformation. When love ends, it forces us to confront our deepest fears and insecurities, to grapple with the rawness of our emotions, and to seek out the hidden lessons within a broken heart.

In the quiet moments after love has ended, when the tears have dried and the world seems still, there is space for reflection. We begin to ask ourselves the tough questions: What did this relationship teach me about love? What has it revealed about my true needs, my limits, my strengths, and my vulnerabilities? These reflections are not easy and require total honesty with ourselves. We must offer ourselves the same compassion we would give to a dear friend in pain.

As we navigate the final stages of lost love, we slowly start to rebuild. We learn to carry the memories with us, not as burdens, but as milestones that guide us toward a deeper understanding of ourselves. The love we once had, though no longer present, has left its mark. It has shaped us, influenced our choices, and enriched our capacity for empathy and connection.

The end of love is not the end of love itself. It is a chapter in the ever, evolving story of our lives, a chapter that paves the way for new beginnings. Through the healing process, we rediscover our resilience, our ability to love again, and our capacity to find joy in the small things in life. We learn that the heart, though scarred, can still be a vessel of love, compassion, and hope.

In time, we come to understand that the end of love is not a failure, but an essential part of the human experience. It teaches us about impermanence, letting go, and the beauty of vulnerability. When love ends, it offers us the opportunity to begin anew, with a deeper self, awareness and a renewed commitment to living a life full of love, love for others, but most importantly, love for ourselves.

Chapter 5:
Recognizing Unhealthy Patterns

Unhealthy patterns can be subtle and insidious, often leading us down a path of emotional turmoil and dissatisfaction. In this chapter, we will explore common signs that can hinder our emotional growth and prevent us from finding true happiness and fulfillment in our lives and relationships. By recognizing these symptoms, we can begin to break free from their grip and create healthier, more balanced lives.

The Cycle of Toxic Relationships

One of the most common unhealthy patterns we may find ourselves caught in is the cycle of toxic relationships. These relationships are characterized by repetitive patterns of emotional abuse, manipulation, and control, often leaving us feeling drained, confused, and questioning our self, worth. Recognizing the signs of a toxic relationship is crucial:

- **Constant Criticism and Belittling:** Frequent put, downs and comments that undermine your self, esteem.

- **Manipulative Behavior and Gaslighting:** Attempts to control your perception of reality, making you doubt your feelings and experiences.

- **Isolation from Friends and Family:** Encouraging or forcing you to cut ties with your support network.

- **Explosive Anger and Emotional Outbursts:** Unpredictable episodes of anger that keep you walking on eggshells.

- **Unpredictable Mood Swings:** Sudden and unexplained changes in behavior and attitude.

- **Blaming and Shifting Responsibility:** Refusing to take accountability and placing the blame on you.

Understanding these signs helps us realize that we deserve better and have the power to break free from toxic dynamics. It can be challenging to let go, especially if this behavior has become normalized over time, but true healing begins when we prioritize our well, being.

The Vicious Cycle of Self, Sabotage

Self, sabotage is another pattern that hinders personal growth, often stemming from deep, seated feelings of unworthiness and a fear of success. We may engage in behaviors that undermine our potential for happiness and fulfillment, consciously or subconsciously.

Signs of self, sabotage include:

- **Procrastination and Avoidance:** Putting off important tasks and opportunities due to fear of failure or change.

- **Negative Self, Talk and Self, Criticism:** Constantly doubting your abilities and worth, reinforcing a negative self, image.

- **Setting Unrealistic Expectations:** Creating impossible standards that set you up for failure and disappointment.

- **Fear of Failure or Success:** Avoiding risks due to fear of either failing or succeeding and facing increased expectations.

- **Self, Sabotaging Relationships or Career Choices:** Engaging in behaviors that undermine your relationships or career growth.

- **Engaging in Self, Destructive Habits:** Turning to harmful coping mechanisms like substance abuse or self, isolation.

Breaking free from self, sabotage requires self, awareness, self, compassion, and a commitment to change. Challenging these negative beliefs and replacing them with positive affirmations is crucial for overcoming self, sabotaging tendencies and embracing a life filled with purpose and fulfillment.

The Perfectionism Trap

Perfectionism is the relentless pursuit of flawlessness and the fear of making mistakes or being judged, often leading to chronic stress, anxiety, and dissatisfaction. This unhealthy pattern can prevent us from experiencing true happiness and self, acceptance.

Common signs of perfectionism include:

- **Setting Impossibly High Standards:** Constantly striving for perfection and feeling like nothing is ever good enough.

- **Intense Anxiety and Fear of Failure:** Paralyzing fear of making mistakes or being judged by others.

- **Being Overly Critical of Yourself and Others:** Harsh self, judgment and unrealistic expectations for others.

- **Avoiding Taking Risks or Trying New Things:** Preferring to stay in the comfort zone to avoid failure.

- **Difficulty Accepting Compliments or Praise:** Feeling uncomfortable or unworthy of recognition.

- **Feeling Overwhelmed by the Need for Control:** An obsessive need to control every aspect of life to avoid imperfection.

Breaking free from perfectionism involves embracing imperfection and practicing self, compassion. It's essential to let go of unrealistic expectations and celebrate progress rather than perfection. Accepting ourselves as we are, flaws and all, allows us to cultivate self, love and create a life filled with joy and authenticity.

Moving Forward

Recognizing unhealthy patterns is the first step toward breaking free from their grip. It takes courage and self, reflection to acknowledge these patterns and commit to change. By being mindful of our thoughts, behaviors, and choices, we can create healthier, more fulfilling lives.

Healing and personal growth are ongoing journeys. It is essential to be patient and kind to yourself as you navigate these changes. Take a moment to reflect on the patterns that resonate with you and consider the steps you can take to begin breaking free. Remember, you have the power to create a life filled with love, joy, and emotional balance!

Codependency: Signs and Solutions

Codependency is a complex issue that often originates from early life experiences or dysfunctional relationships. It is characterized by an excessive reliance on others for validation, a lack of personal boundaries, and an inability to prioritize one's own needs. Understanding the signs of codependency and learning how to overcome them is essential for developing healthier, more balanced relationships.

Signs of Codependency

1. **Difficulty Saying "No" or Setting Boundaries:**

    People struggling with codependency often have difficulty saying "no," fearing rejection or disapproval. This can lead to situations where they feel taken advantage of, as they prioritize others' needs over their own. The inability to set boundaries often stems from a desire to please others and maintain their approval.

2. **Feeling Responsible for Others' Emotions or Actions:**

   Codependent individuals frequently feel responsible for the emotions or behaviors of those around them. They might believe it is their duty to solve problems or alleviate the distress of others, often at the expense of their well, being. This behavior is often driven by a need to feel needed or indispensable in relationships.

3. **Prioritizing Others' Needs Above Their Own:**

   A key characteristic of codependency is consistently placing others' needs above one's own, leading to emotional exhaustion and burnout. This behavior is typically rooted in the belief that one's worth is tied to their ability to care for and support others.

4. **Sense of Emptiness or Worthlessness Without External Validation:**

   Codependent individuals often struggle with low self, esteem and a pervasive sense of emptiness when they are not receiving validation from others. This can lead to a cycle of seeking approval and validation from external sources to feel valued and worthy.

5. **Difficulty Expressing Personal Emotions or Needs:**

   Expressing personal emotions and needs can be challenging for those with codependency. They may fear that being honest about their feelings will lead to rejection or conflict, so they suppress their emotions, leading to internal stress and dissatisfaction.

6. **Fear of Abandonment or Rejection:**

   Codependency often involves an intense fear of being abandoned or rejected. This fear can drive individuals to cling to unhealthy relationships, even when they are damaging, because the idea of being alone feels more terrifying.

7. **Enabling or Rescuing Others from Their Problems:**

   Codependent individuals may take on the role of rescuer, often enabling destructive behaviors in others in an attempt to feel needed and important. This dynamic can perpetuate unhealthy patterns in relationships and prevent both parties from growing.

8. **Seeking Approval and Validation from Others:**

   Seeking constant approval and validation from others is a hallmark of codependency. This behavior stems from a lack of internal self, worth and the belief that one's value is contingent upon others' perceptions and approval.

Solutions for Overcoming Codependency

1. **Cultivate Self, Awareness:**

   Developing self, awareness is essential for addressing codependency. By becoming more aware of your own needs, emotions, and boundaries, you can begin to understand the patterns driving your behavior. Tools such as journaling, therapy, and self, reflection can help you identify and address these patterns.

2. **Set Healthy Boundaries:**

   Learning to set clear and healthy boundaries is critical for overcoming codependency. Practice asserting your needs and saying "no" when necessary. Establishing boundaries is an act of self, respect and self, care, essential for maintaining your emotional and mental well, being.

3. **Prioritize Self, Care:**

   Make self, care a priority in your life by engaging in activities that bring you joy, relaxation, and fulfillment. Regular self, care strengthens your emotional resilience and reinforces the importance of taking care of yourself first.

4. **Develop Healthy Communication Skills:**

   Improving communication skills can help you express your emotions and needs more effectively. Practice active listening, empathy, and assertiveness to foster healthier and more balanced relationships.

5. **Build a Supportive Network:**

   Surround yourself with positive, supportive individuals who encourage your growth and well, being. A supportive network can provide the necessary emotional support as you work to overcome codependency. Joining support groups can also offer valuable insights and shared experiences.

6. **Challenge Limiting Beliefs:**

   Challenge the limiting beliefs that contribute to codependent behaviors. Replace negative self, talk with positive affirmations and cultivate a strong, positive self, image. Recognize that you deserve love, respect, and healthy relationships, and that your value is not dependent on others' approval.

7. **Practice Self, Love and Self, Care:**

   Developing a healthy relationship with yourself is key to overcoming codependency. Engage in practices that promote self, acceptance, self, compassion, and self, discovery. Treat yourself with the same kindness and compassion you would offer to someone you care about.

8. **Seek Professional Help:**

   If codependency is deeply ingrained or causing significant distress, consider seeking professional help. Therapists or counselors can provide guidance, support, and specialized techniques to help you address and overcome codependent patterns.

Moving Forward

Implementing these strategies and seeking support when needed can help you overcome codependent behaviors, create healthier relationships, and cultivate emotional balance in your life. Remember, codependency is not a permanent state, it is a learned behavior that can be unlearned, allowing you to live a more fulfilled and balanced life.

Understanding Emotional Dependency

Emotional dependency is a condition where we excessively rely on others to satisfy our emotional needs and seek validation. This state undermines our self, esteem and creates a sense of inner emptiness that only external recognition seems to fill. While the need for emotional connection is natural and universal, emotional dependency becomes problematic when it leads to a lack of emotional autonomy, causing us to live under the influence of others' reactions and judgments.

The Roots of Emotional Dependency

Emotional dependency often has its roots in childhood, stemming from formative experiences such as inconsistent emotional support or a traumatic upbringing that prevents the development of a strong sense of self. Children raised in environments where their emotions are neglected, invalidated, or ignored may grow up with deep emotional insecurities. As adults, they may try to fill this void by relying on others to meet their emotional needs.

Unresolved emotional traumas can foster this condition, creating a pattern where the need for acceptance and external approval takes precedence over emotional self, sufficiency. While dependency on others may provide temporary comfort, it ultimately perpetuates a cycle of insecurity and neediness.

The Cycle of Emotional Dependency

Emotional dependency often follows a repetitive cycle that reinforces the need for validation and emotional support from others. This cycle can be broken down into four stages:

1. **Idealization:**

    In this stage, we place others on a pedestal, believing they hold the key to our happiness and emotional well, being. We become infatuated and develop an intense need for their presence and approval.

2. **Clinging:**

    As idealization deepens, we begin to depend heavily on the person we idealize, constantly seeking their attention and reassurance. Our happiness becomes tied to their presence, leading to anxiety and insecurity when they are not around.

3. **Disillusionment:**

    Inevitably, the person we idealize falls short of our expectations. They cannot fulfill all our emotional needs or live up to the pedestal we've placed them on. This stage often leads to disappointment, frustration, and a sense of betrayal.

4. **Withdrawal:**

   In this final stage, we experience withdrawal symptoms similar to those felt when breaking free from an addiction. Intense loneliness, sadness, and a deep longing for the person we depended on take hold. Breaking free from this cycle requires self, reflection, self, compassion, and a commitment to personal growth.

The Impact of Emotional Dependency

Emotional dependency can significantly impact our well, being and relationships. It can lead to:

- **Codependency:**

  Emotional dependency often coexists with codependency, where we prioritize others' needs over our own. This imbalance prevents self, care and healthy boundaries, making it difficult to foster fulfilling relationships.

- **Low Self, Esteem:**

  Relying on others for self, worth erodes self, esteem and confidence. We may constantly seek validation, feeling inadequate without it.

- **Unhealthy Relationships:**

Emotional dependency fosters unbalanced and unhealthy relationships. We may attract partners who reinforce our dependency, perpetuating a cycle of emotional pain and dissatisfaction.

- **Stunted Personal Growth:**

When our emotional well, being depends on others, we limit our personal growth. Fear of rejection or abandonment may stop us from taking risks, setting boundaries, or pursuing our passions.

Breaking Free from Emotional Dependency

Breaking free from emotional dependency requires, as in previous cases, self, awareness, self, compassion, and a commitment to personal growth. Here are some steps you can take to start your journey toward emotional independence:

1. **Self, Reflection:**

    Take time to reflect on your patterns of emotional dependency and the underlying causes that fuel them. This self, exploration will help you understand why you excessively seek validation and support from others.

2. **Cultivate Self, Love:**

    Focus on developing a healthy sense of self, worth. Practice self, care, set boundaries, and prioritize your needs and desires. Remember, loving yourself is a prerequisite for healthy relationships with others.

3. **Build a Supportive Network:**

   Surround yourself with people who uplift and support you. Cultivate relationships based on mutual respect, trust, and emotional support, which will provide a foundation for your emotional growth.

4. **Develop Emotional Resilience:**

   Work on building emotional resilience to handle challenges independently. Practice self, soothing techniques like mindfulness and self, compassion to strengthen your ability to cope with difficult emotions.

5. **Seek Professional Help:**

   If emotional dependency is deeply ingrained and affecting your daily life, consider seeking help from a therapist or counselor. They can provide personalized strategies and support on your journey toward emotional independence.

By recognizing the cycle of emotional dependency, understanding its impact, and taking proactive steps toward personal growth, you can create a fulfilling life, nurture healthy relationships, and achieve emotional balance.

Case Study: Breaking Free from Toxic Relationships

Breaking free from toxic relationships can be a challenging and emotionally exhausting process. Here's a real, life example that illustrates this journey.

Emily's Story: Escaping the Cycle of Abuse

Emily was a strong and determined woman, known for her resilience and ability to face any challenge. However, despite her inner strength, she found herself trapped in a relationship that, over time, took a devastating toll on her self, esteem and emotional well, being.

Her relationship with Mark began like many others, filled with tenderness and promises of everlasting love. At first, Mark seemed caring and affectionate, attentive to every detail of Emily's life. But slowly, his behavior began to change. He became possessive, controlling every aspect of Emily's life, from her friendships to her daily decisions.

Mark isolated her, under the guise of protecting her from the outside world, making her believe that no one else could understand her like he did. Emily, in love and eager to maintain peace in the relationship, began to give in and comply, distancing herself from friends and family. Her closest friendships were cast into doubt, and her bond with her family grew cold.

Every day, Mark ensured that Emily felt less and less secure about herself, undermining her self, esteem with subtle yet constant criticisms. He made her feel inadequate, suggesting she wasn't good enough, smart enough, or beautiful enough to deserve anyone's love. These words, repeated day after day, became an invisible prison for Emily, one that seemed impossible to escape.

As the years went by, the emotional abuse began to manifest physically as well. Emily found herself living in a constant state of fear, dreading Mark's reactions to her every move. Her vitality seemed to vanish, replaced by a sense of powerlessness and despair. But deep down, her inner strength hadn't completely disappeared; it was just waiting for the right moment to reemerge.

That glimmer of hope came through an old friend who managed to reconnect with Emily. This friend, seeing the pain hidden behind Emily's forced smile, decided to help her find a way out. With their support, Emily began to recognize the abuse she was enduring and found the courage to fight back.

After a long period of emotional and logistical preparation, Emily made the hardest decision of her life: to leave Mark. She sought therapy to address the trauma she had experienced and began a journey of personal rebuilding, learning to rediscover her worth and independence.

Today, Emily has not only survived but has flourished. Her story is a powerful example of how, even in the darkest situations, it is possible to find the strength to break free, thanks to the support of loved ones and the determination not to be defeated. Her experience reminds us that no one should ever accept living in an abusive situation and that there is always a way out, no matter how difficult it may seem.

Recognizing the Signs of Toxic Relationships

One of the first steps toward breaking free from a toxic relationship is recognizing the signs of toxicity. Here are some common indicators:

- **Physical or emotional abuse:** This can include verbal insults, threats, physical violence, or controlling behaviors.

- **Isolation:** The toxic partner may try to isolate you from friends and family, making you dependent on them for support and validation.

- **Manipulation:** Toxic individuals often use manipulation tactics to control and undermine your self, esteem.

- **Lack of respect:** They may disregard your boundaries, dismiss your opinions, or constantly criticize you.

- **Unequal power dynamics:** Toxic relationships are often characterized by an imbalance of power, with one partner exerting control over the other.

Recognizing these signs is crucial to taking the necessary steps toward breaking free from toxicity and reclaiming your emotional well, being.

Creating an Exit Plan

Leaving a toxic relationship requires careful planning to ensure your safety and minimize potential harm. Here are some steps to consider when creating an exit plan:

- **Seek support:** Reach out to trusted friends, family members, or professionals who can provide emotional support and guidance.

- **Ensure your safety:** If you feel unsafe, consider contacting local authorities or organizations that specialize in domestic violence.

- **Financial independence:** Start building financial independence by opening a separate bank account and saving money whenever possible.

- **Document evidence:** Keep a record of any incidents of abuse or manipulation, such as text messages, emails, or photographs, as evidence if needed.

- **Develop a support network:** Surround yourself with positive influences who can provide emotional support and help you stay focused on your goal of breaking free.

Creating an exit plan is a crucial step toward breaking free from toxicity. It helps ensure your safety and provides a clear roadmap for your journey toward healing and self, discovery.

Rebuilding Self, Worth and Establishing Boundaries

After leaving a toxic relationship, it is essential to focus on rebuilding your self, worth and establishing healthy boundaries. Here are some strategies to help you on this path:

- **Practice self, compassion:** Be kind and forgiving to yourself as you heal from the emotional wounds inflicted by the toxic relationship.

- **Seek professional help:** Consider working with a therapist or counselor who specializes in trauma and relationship issues.

- **Engage in self, care:** Prioritize activities that bring you joy and promote your well, being, such as exercise, meditation, or pursuing hobbies.

- **Set clear boundaries:** Clearly communicate your boundaries to others and enforce them to prevent toxic individuals from entering your life.

- **Surround yourself with positivity:** Surround yourself with supportive and loving individuals who uplift and inspire you.

Remember, rebuilding self, worth is a gradual process, but with time and effort, you can cultivate a healthy sense of self and establish boundaries that protect your emotional well, being.

Moving Forward: Embracing Healthy Relationships

Breaking free from toxic relationships opens the door to the possibility of healthy, loving connections. Here are some key principles to keep in mind as you navigate new relationships:

- **Know your worth:** Recognize your own value and never settle for anything less than the respect and love you deserve.

- **Communicate openly:** Foster open and honest communication with your partner, sharing your thoughts, needs, and concerns.

- **Trust your instincts:** Listen to your gut instincts and pay attention to any red flags that may indicate potential toxicity.

- **Practice self, love:** Prioritize self, care and self, love, nurturing your own well, being before seeking validation from others.

- **Take it slow:** Allow relationships to develop naturally, taking the time to truly get to know your partner before fully committing.

Important: Embracing healthy relationships is a transformative journey that requires self, awareness, self, love, and a commitment to personal growth. It is a journey well worth taking.

Breaking free from toxic relationships is a courageous act that paves the way for personal growth, emotional healing, and the pursuit of healthy, fulfilling connections. By recognizing the signs of toxicity, creating an exit plan, rebuilding self, worth, and embracing healthy relationships, you can embark on a transformative journey toward emotional balance and self, discovery.

Chapter 6:
Acceptance and Closure

Few experiences in life test our emotional resilience as profoundly as the need to find acceptance and closure after a significant loss or the end of an important relationship. Whether it's a breakup, the loss of a loved one, or the conclusion of a significant chapter in your life, acceptance and closure are crucial for healing and moving forward.

In this chapter, we explore the essential journey of making peace with the past and finding inner serenity. Acceptance doesn't mean forgetting or diminishing the significance of what you've lost or experienced. Instead, it's about acknowledging the reality of the situation and allowing yourself to move forward with love and compassion for yourself. It's an act of recognizing the truth of what has happened and choosing to release the pain and regret that may linger.

Understanding Acceptance as a Process

Acceptance is not a destination; it's a process, one that often requires time and patience. Many people feel pressure to "move on" within a certain timeframe, but healing doesn't follow a set schedule. Each person's journey towards acceptance is unique, shaped by their individual experiences and the nature of their loss. It's important to give yourself the grace to experience this process at your own pace, without self, judgment.

Throughout this chapter, we will explore different stages of this journey, helping you identify where you are in the process and providing guidance on how to navigate each phase with compassion and understanding.

Exploring the Concept of Closure

Closure is often thought of as a definitive ending, a sense that everything has been resolved, and it's time to turn the page. However, closure is not always about finding concrete answers or having a final conversation. For some, closure is an internal and emotional process, a personal reconciliation with the past through self, reflection and understanding.

This chapter will provide insights into how to seek closure in a way that is healthy and constructive. Whether through communication, reflective practices, or creating new beginnings, you will find strategies to help you reach a place of peace. Closure doesn't mean forgetting or dismissing your feelings; it means integrating your experiences into your life in a way that allows you to grow and thrive.

Embracing Emotions as Part of Healing

As you navigate this chapter, you will be encouraged to embrace whatever emotions arise, be it sadness, anger, or even relief. These emotions are a natural part of the healing process, and acknowledging them is a fundamental step toward acceptance. You will find practical strategies to help you address these feelings, including mindfulness practices, reflective writing exercises, and techniques for cultivating self, compassion.

Tools for Finding Acceptance and Closure

This chapter will guide you through various practical tools and strategies designed to help you move forward in a way that honors your experiences. Here are a few techniques we will explore:

- **Mindfulness Practices:** Learn to be present with your emotions without judgment, allowing yourself to experience them fully and let go of resistance.

- **Reflective Writing Exercises:** Use journaling to explore your thoughts and feelings, helping you gain clarity and insight into your healing process.

- **Self, Compassion Techniques:** Develop self, compassion to treat yourself with the kindness and understanding you would offer to a friend.

The goal is not merely to move past the pain, but to equip you with the tools to do so in a way that respects your journey and strengthens your resilience.

Acceptance and Closure as Acts of Self, Love

Remember, acceptance and closure are profound acts of self, love. They are gifts you give yourself to heal, grow, and open up to new possibilities. By allowing yourself to find peace with the past, you make room for joy, love, and fulfillment in the future. As you journey through this chapter, keep in mind that every step you take towards acceptance and closure is a step towards a brighter, more empowered version of yourself.

Strategies for Acceptance

Acceptance is often perceived as a passive process, but in reality, it is an active and dynamic journey. It involves a conscious choice to acknowledge the reality of a situation, embrace the emotions that come with it, and ultimately move forward with a sense of peace. In this section, we will explore various strategies that can help you cultivate acceptance, especially after experiencing loss, heartbreak, or significant life changes. These strategies are not one, size, fits, all; instead, they represent a toolkit from which you can choose the practices that resonate most with your personal healing journey.

1. **Mindfulness and Present, Moment Awareness**

    One of the most powerful tools for cultivating acceptance is mindfulness. Mindfulness involves staying present and fully engaged in the current moment without judgment. It encourages you to observe your thoughts and feelings as they arise, rather than pushing them away or becoming overwhelmed by them.

By practicing mindfulness, you can learn to sit with uncomfortable emotions like pain, anger, or sadness without trying to change or escape these feelings. This practice reduces the hold these emotions have over you, allowing you to experience them fully without being consumed by them. Over time, mindfulness fosters a more compassionate and welcoming attitude toward your own emotional experiences.

To integrate mindfulness into your daily life, consider starting with short guided meditations focused on breath awareness or body scanning. These practices can help you build the habit of regularly checking in with yourself, fostering greater self, awareness and acceptance.

2. Reframing Thoughts and Challenging Negative Beliefs

Acceptance often requires a shift in perspective. Reframing is a cognitive, behavioral strategy that involves identifying and challenging negative or unhelpful thoughts, then replacing them with more constructive ones. This process can help you move from a place of resistance and denial to one of acceptance and confidence.

For instance, if you find yourself stuck in a cycle of self-blame after a relationship ends, try reframing the situation. Instead of thinking, "It's all my fault," consider, "I did my best, and there were factors beyond my control." Reframing doesn't mean ignoring your emotions but rather allows you to view the situation from different angles, often leading to a more compassionate outlook.

3. Journaling for Reflection and Emotional Release

Keeping a journal is a powerful way to process emotions and gain clarity on your thoughts and feelings. When it comes to acceptance, journaling can serve as a safe space to explore the complexities of your emotions and to document your healing journey.

Writing about your experiences helps you make sense of them, identify patterns in your thinking, and recognize your progress. It also provides an opportunity for emotional release, allowing you to express feelings that you might find difficult to articulate otherwise.

To get started, consider using guiding questions such as:

- What does acceptance mean to me in this situation?
- What emotions am I struggling to accept?

- What steps can I take to move closer to acceptance?

Revisiting your journal entries can help you track your progress and reinforce the sense that you are moving forward, even if the journey sometimes feels slow or challenging.

4. Self, Compassion: Being Kind to Yourself

Self, compassion is essential to acceptance. It means treating yourself with the same kindness and understanding you would offer to a dear friend in a similar situation. Practicing self, compassion allows you to acknowledge that suffering, failure, and imperfection are part of the human experience, enabling you to be gentle with yourself during difficult times.

The three core components of self, compassion are:

- **Self, kindness:** Being warm and understanding toward yourself when you suffer, fail, or feel inadequate.

- **Common humanity:** Recognizing that suffering and personal shortcomings are part of the shared human experience.

- **Mindfulness:** Holding your painful thoughts and feelings in balanced awareness, rather than ignoring or exaggerating them.

By cultivating self, compassion, you can reduce feelings of guilt, shame, or self, criticism that may hinder your ability to accept a difficult situation. This approach fosters a more forgiving and nurturing attitude, making it easier to embrace acceptance.

5. Creating Rituals for Closure

Rituals can be a meaningful way to symbolize acceptance and closure. Whether you are grieving a loss, moving on from a relationship, or closing a chapter in your life, rituals can provide a sense of finality and help you transition into the next phase of your life.

These rituals don't have to be elaborate; they can be as simple as writing a letter to the person or situation you are letting go of and then symbolically releasing it, perhaps by burning the letter, burying it, or setting it adrift in water. The act of performing a ritual can help you externalize your internal process, providing a tangible way to mark the shift from one phase to another.

You might also create a ritual around self, care, such as lighting a candle each evening as a reminder to check in with yourself and practice self, compassion. Rituals provide structure and a sense of purpose, helping to anchor you as you navigate the complexities of acceptance.

6. Seeking Support: Therapy and Community

Acceptance is an internal process, but it doesn't have to be solitary. Seeking support from a therapist, counselor, or support group can be invaluable in helping you navigate the emotions and challenges that arise during this journey.

Therapy offers a safe space to explore your feelings, gain insights into your patterns of thinking, and develop strategies for acceptance. A therapist can also help you work through resistance and offer guidance as you move forward.

Support groups, whether in, person or online, provide the opportunity to connect with others who are going through similar experiences. Sharing your story and hearing others' experiences can provide comfort, reduce feelings of isolation, and offer new perspectives on the process of acceptance.

7. Practicing Gratitude and Positive Affirmations

Gratitude and positive affirmations play a significant role in shifting your mindset toward acceptance. By focusing on what you're grateful for, whether it's your health, family, or material possessions, you can cultivate a sense of appreciation for the positives in your life, even during difficult times.

Keeping a gratitude journal, where you regularly note the things you are thankful for, can help reframe your perspective. Similarly, positive affirmations, statements that reinforce positive beliefs about yourself and your situation, can counteract negative thinking and foster acceptance.

Examples of affirmations might include:

- *"I am strong enough to accept and overcome this situation."*

- *"I deserve love and happiness."*

- *"I believe in myself and my ability to move forward."*

Repeating these affirmations regularly can reinforce your commitment to acceptance and create a more positive internal dialogue.

8. Embracing Change and Letting Go

Acceptance often requires a willingness to embrace change and let go of the past. This can be one of the most challenging aspects of the process, as it involves releasing attachments to people, situations, or outcomes that you once held dear.

Letting go doesn't mean forgetting your experiences; it's about freeing yourself from the grip of what no longer serves you. It's about making space for new experiences, relationships, and opportunities that align with your current needs and values.

Reflection, meditation, and the conscious decision to focus on the present and future, rather than dwelling on the past, can facilitate this process. It may also involve setting new goals that reflect your growth and the lessons you've learned.

9. Integrating Acceptance into Daily Life

Acceptance is not a one, time event but a practice to be integrated into daily life. It means continuously choosing to accept yourself, your emotions, and your circumstances while also striving for growth and positive change.

By incorporating acceptance into your daily routine, through mindfulness, gratitude, self, compassion, or other strategies, you can create a foundation of emotional resilience that supports you in facing life's challenges with grace and balance.

The journey toward acceptance is deeply personal and transformative. It requires patience, self, compassion, and a commitment to growth. By exploring and applying these strategies, you can cultivate a greater sense of peace and resilience, allowing you to face life's challenges with confidence and clarity. Acceptance isn't about giving up or resigning yourself to a situation; it's about embracing reality with an open heart and mind and allowing yourself to move forward with strength and hope.

The Importance of Closure

Closure is a fundamental yet often overlooked aspect of the healing process following a significant emotional event, such as the end of a relationship, the loss of a loved one, or a major life transition. Without closure, unresolved emotions and unanswered questions can linger, potentially hindering your ability to move forward and find peace. Eventually, it becomes necessary to put a period on the past and close that chapter.

What is Closure?

Closure is the sense of resolution or conclusion that occurs when you can make peace with a past event, relationship, or chapter of your life. It involves understanding and accepting what happened and why it happened, allowing yourself to move on without being tethered to the past by unresolved emotions, questions, or regrets. For many, closure does not mean completely forgetting or erasing the past, but rather finding a way to integrate that experience into your life story without causing ongoing pain or discomfort.

It's the emotional and psychological process of tying up loose ends, both internally and externally, so that you can step forward into the future with a sense of peace, serenity, and clarity.

Why Closure Is Important

- **Emotional Healing:**

    One of the most significant benefits of achieving closure is emotional healing. Without that sense of finality, of putting it all behind, you may find unresolved emotions like anger, sadness, or regret continuing to disturb your mental and emotional state. These lingering feelings can prevent you from fully healing and may even manifest as physical symptoms such as stress, anxiety, or depression. Achieving closure helps you process these emotions, understand them, and ultimately release them, leading to greater emotional well, being.

- **Moving Forward:**

    Closure is essential for moving forward in life. When you hold on to the past, it can be difficult to embrace new opportunities, relationships, and experiences. Closure allows you to let go of what was and make space for what can be. It frees you from the grip of the past and opens the door to growth, evolution, and the possibility of embarking on new paths with clarity and confidence.

- **Self, Understanding and Growth:**

   Seeking closure often involves deep reflection and introspection, which can lead to greater self, understanding and personal growth. By examining what happened, why it happened, and how it affected you, you can gain valuable insights into your behavior patterns, beliefs, and emotional responses. This understanding can serve as a powerful catalyst for growth, helping you learn from past experiences and make more informed choices in the future.

- **Restoring Balance and Peace:**

   Unresolved issues can create a continuous sense of imbalance or unease in your life. Without closure, you might find yourself ruminating on the past, replaying events in your mind, and struggling to find peace. Achieving closure helps restore balance by allowing you to put the past to rest and focus on the present, where you have the power to shape your future. It brings a deep sense of peace and calm, knowing that you have dealt with what needed to be dealt with and can now move forward without being weighed down by unresolved issues.

- **Improving Future Relationships:**

When you can put a definitive end to past relationships, whether romantic, familial, or friendships, it positively impacts your future connections. Unresolved issues from the past can spill over into new relationships, creating tension, mistrust, or unhealthy behavior patterns. Closure helps you heal from past wounds, learn from your experiences, and enter new relationships with a healthier, more balanced mindset.

How to Seek and Create Closure

- **Acceptance of Reality:**

The first step toward closure is accepting the reality of the situation. This can be one of the most challenging aspects, as it often requires letting go of hopes, dreams, or expectations tied to the past. Acceptance doesn't mean you're happy about what happened, but rather that you recognize it for what it is and are willing to face it directly. By accepting reality, you can begin to process your emotions and move closer to closure, starting your "rebirth."

- **Self, Reflection and Understanding:**

Take time to reflect on what happened, how it affected you, and why. This can include journaling, meditation, or talking with a trusted friend or therapist. Ask yourself questions like: *What can I learn from this experience? How did it change me? What do I need to let go of?* This reflection can help you gain a deeper understanding of the situation and your role in it, which is essential for finding closure and inner peace.

- **Communication and Expression:**

    In some cases, closure may involve a conversation with the person involved in the situation. This could be a way to express your feelings, ask questions, or gain a better understanding of their perspective. However, this is not always possible or advisable, depending on the circumstances. If direct communication isn't an option, you can still express your thoughts and feelings by writing a letter (even if you don't send it), talking with a therapist, or through a creative outlet like art or music. The important thing is to find a way to express and process your emotions rather than keeping them bottled up inside.

- **Creating a Ritual for Closure:**

    Rituals can be a powerful way to symbolize the act of letting go and moving on. This could be as simple as writing down your thoughts and feelings and then burning the paper, letting it go in the wind, or burying it as a symbol of putting the past to rest. Some people find closure through ceremonies, such as lighting a candle in memory of a loved one or creating a piece of art that represents their journey. The act of performing a ritual can help you externalize your internal process and give you a tangible way to mark the transition from holding on to letting go.

- **Forgiveness:**

  Forgiveness is often a crucial part of achieving closure, whether it involves forgiving others or yourself. Holding on to resentment, anger, or guilt can prevent you from finding peace and moving forward. Forgiveness does not mean condoning what happened or forgetting it; rather, it means releasing the hold these negative emotions have on you. It's about freeing yourself from the burden of carrying these emotions, allowing you to move forward with a lighter heart and a clearer mind.

- **Letting Go of the Need for Answers:**

  Sometimes, closure is difficult because we feel the need to have all the answers or to understand everything that happened. However, life is not always clear, cut, and there are times when we may never fully understand why something happened. Letting go of the need for answers can be an important step in finding closure. It involves trusting that you can still move forward without having everything neatly resolved and being okay with the uncertainty that sometimes accompanies closure.

- **Seeking Professional Help:**

If you're struggling to find closure on your own, it may be helpful to seek the guidance of a therapist or counselor. A professional can provide you with tools and strategies to work through your emotions, help you gain perspective, and support you on your journey toward closure. They can also help you address any underlying issues that may be making it difficult for you to move on.

- **Embracing the New Beginning:**

Closure is not just about ending something; it is also about beginning something new. Once you have gone through the process of closure, take time to focus on what comes next. Set new goals, explore new opportunities, and embrace the possibilities that the future offers. Closure can be a doorway to growth and new experiences, allowing you to move forward with a renewed sense of purpose and direction.

Remember:

Closure is not about erasing the past but about integrating it into your life story in a way that allows you to grow and thrive. It's a gift you give yourself, a way to honor your experiences while making room for the new and the unknown. By seeking and creating closure, you open the door to a future full of possibilities, healing, and growth. Believe in yourself and in the process!

Exercise:
Writing a Closure Letter

Writing a closure letter is a powerful and transformative tool for achieving inner peace and letting go of the past. This exercise provides you with a safe space to express your thoughts and feelings in a structured way, helping you to process and release unresolved emotions. It is a crucial step toward acceptance, healing, and creating space for new beginnings.

Instructions:

1. **Set Your Intention:**

   Before you begin writing, take a moment to reflect on your intention. What do you hope to achieve with this letter? Do you want to find peace, release anger, or gain clarity? Setting a clear intention will guide your writing and keep you focused on your healing journey.

2. **Express Your Emotions Freely:**

   Begin your letter by acknowledging and validating your emotions. Allow yourself to be completely honest about how you feel regarding the situation or person. This is your chance to voice everything you've been holding back, anger, sadness, disappointment, or even gratitude. Remember, no emotion is too small or unimportant. This is your space to be completely honest with yourself.

3. **Reflect on the Experience:**

   Take a moment to look back on what happened. What did this experience teach you? What did you learn about yourself, your needs, and your boundaries? Acknowledge the pain and any disappointments, but also recognize the strengths and lessons you have gained. This reflection will help you reframe the experience as part of your personal growth journey.

4. **Declare Your Closure:**

   Conclude your letter by stating your intention to let go and move forward. Use affirmations like, "I choose to release this situation and move on," or "I give myself permission to let go and create a new chapter in my life." This declaration is a symbolic act of reclaiming your power and setting yourself free.

5. **Decide the Fate of the Letter:**

   Once you have written your letter, decide what feels most liberating for you. You can keep the letter as a personal reminder of your decision, destroy it as a symbolic gesture of release, or store it in a safe place where you can revisit it if needed. The choice is yours, do what feels most healing and empowering for you.

This exercise is a powerful way to externalize your internal process, offering a sense of finality and helping you move forward with greater peace and clarity. Remember, closure is not about forgetting, but about integrating your experiences in a way that allows you to grow and thrive.

Chapter 7:
Healing a Broken Heart

In this chapter, we will explore the deeply personal and often challenging journey of healing a broken heart. Heartbreak can leave us feeling lost, vulnerable, and overwhelmed, but with the right tools and support, it is possible to mend these emotional wounds and emerge stronger than before. We will delve into a variety of techniques and strategies that can help you navigate this difficult time, providing guidance and support as you rebuild your emotional strength and resilience.

The healing process is unique to each individual, and there is no one, size, fits, all approach. However, understanding and utilizing the different tools available can offer valuable assistance. The first section of this chapter will focus on practical techniques for emotional healing. It is essential to acknowledge your pain and allow yourself to grieve. Suppressing or denying your emotions can prolong the healing process and intensify your suffering. Instead, embrace your feelings and give yourself permission to experience them fully.

Techniques such as journaling, meditation, and mindfulness are powerful methods for exploring and releasing the emotions tied to your heartbreak. Journaling can help you articulate your thoughts and emotions, offering clarity and insight. Meditation and mindfulness practices allow you to stay present and observe your feelings without judgment, fostering a sense of peace and acceptance.

One of the most crucial aspects of healing is having a strong support system. In times of emotional turmoil, the presence of friends, family, or even a therapist can be invaluable. This chapter will emphasize the importance of not isolating yourself during the healing process. Instead, lean on those who care about you and can provide comfort, understanding, and perspective. Whether you seek professional help, join a support group, or spend time with loved ones, having a network of support can make a significant difference in your recovery journey.

Finally, this chapter includes a guided reflection exercise designed to help you process your emotions and gain clarity on your healing path. Reflection is a powerful tool that allows you to explore your pain, identify patterns, and develop a deeper sense of self, awareness. Through guided questions and prompts, you will be encouraged to reflect on your feelings, recognize the lessons learned from your experience, and set intentions for the future. This practice serves as a compass, guiding you through the complexities of heartbreak and helping you find your way back to emotional wholeness.

Remember, healing a broken heart is not about rushing through the pain or pretending it doesn't exist. It's about giving yourself the time and space to feel, to reflect, and to grow. With patience, compassion, and the right support, you can navigate this journey and emerge on the other side with renewed strength and a deeper understanding of yourself.

Techniques for Emotional Healing

Healing from a broken heart is a deeply personal journey that requires time, self, compassion, and the right tools to navigate the emotional turmoil. While the process can feel overwhelming, especially in the initial stages, there are several effective techniques that can support you in managing and eventually healing from the pain. This section delves into various methods that promote emotional healing, offering practical guidance to help you regain your sense of well, being and move forward with renewed strength.

1. **Journaling: A Safe Space for Emotional Expression**

    Journaling is one of the most accessible and effective tools for emotional healing. It provides a private, non, judgmental space where you can freely express your thoughts and feelings. Writing about your experiences allows you to process complex emotions, identify patterns in your thinking, and gain clarity on your situation.

One approach to journaling is free writing, where you let your thoughts flow onto the page without concern for structure or grammar. This can be particularly cathartic, as it helps to release pent, up emotions and provides a sense of relief. Another approach is guided journaling, using specific prompts to explore certain aspects of your emotional experience. Prompts like "What am I feeling right now?" or "What lessons have I learned from this experience?" can help you focus on understanding your emotions and finding meaning in your journey.

Journaling also serves as a record of your healing progress. Over time, you can look back on your entries and see how far you've come, which can be incredibly empowering and motivating.

2. **Mindfulness and Meditation: Cultivating Present, Moment Awareness**

Mindfulness and meditation are powerful techniques for emotional healing, helping you stay grounded in the present moment rather than being overwhelmed by past wounds or future anxieties. Mindfulness involves paying attention to your thoughts, emotions, and bodily sensations without judgment, teaching you to observe your feelings as they arise, allowing them to pass without clinging to or suppressing them.

Meditation, on the other hand, is a focused practice that helps calm the mind and soothe emotional distress. Techniques like breath awareness, where you focus on the sensation of your breath moving in and out of your body, can help reduce stress and anxiety. Aim to practice for at least 10 minutes, once or even twice a day. Guided meditations focused on self, compassion or emotional healing can also be particularly beneficial, offering a structured approach to addressing and releasing painful emotions.

By incorporating mindfulness and meditation into your daily routine, you can cultivate a greater sense of emotional mastery. These practices, when done consistently, help you build a more compassionate relationship with yourself, reducing the intensity of negative emotions and creating space for healing.

3. Therapy: Professional Support for Deep Healing

Engaging in therapy can be a transformative way to facilitate emotional healing, especially when dealing with complex emotions or past traumas. A therapist provides a safe, supportive environment where you can explore your feelings, gain insights into your behavior, and develop coping strategies.

Cognitive Behavioral Therapy (CBT) helps identify and challenge negative thought patterns, replacing them with healthier, more balanced ways of thinking. **Emotionally Focused Therapy (EFT)** addresses attachment issues and helps process deep, seated emotional wounds. For significant trauma, **Eye Movement Desensitization and Reprocessing (EMDR)** can be particularly beneficial, reprocessing traumatic memories and reducing their emotional impact.

4. Physical Activity: Moving the Body to Heal the Mind

Physical activity not only benefits your body but also plays a crucial role in emotional healing. Exercise releases endorphins, the body's natural "feel, good" chemicals, which can improve your mood and reduce feelings of depression and anxiety.

Engaging in regular physical activity, whether it's running, yoga, dancing, or even just walking, helps you process emotions and reduce stress. Yoga, in particular, combines movement, breathwork, and mindfulness to release tension and promote inner peace. Physical activity also provides a healthy distraction from emotional pain, reminding you of your strength and resilience.

5. Creative Expression: Channeling Emotions Through Art

Creative expression offers a unique and powerful outlet for processing and healing emotions. Engaging in activities like painting, drawing, writing poetry, or playing music allows you to externalize your feelings in a tangible form. This can be particularly helpful when words alone aren't enough to express the depth of your emotions.

Art therapy, a structured form of creative expression, encourages you to explore your feelings through the creative process. Even if you don't consider yourself artistically inclined, creating something can be incredibly therapeutic. It allows you to take control of your emotional narrative and transform pain into something meaningful, helping to rebuild your identity after a breakup.

6. Building a Support System: The Power of Connection

The journey of healing is deeply personal, but it doesn't have to be undertaken alone. Building and relying on a support system is crucial for emotional healing. Whether it's friends, family, or support groups, having people who can listen, offer comfort, and provide perspective can make a significant difference.

Talking about your experiences with others helps you process your emotions and feel less isolated in your pain. Support groups, whether in person or online, offer a space to connect with others who are going through similar experiences. Sharing your story and hearing others' can foster a sense of community and provide strength.

7. Self, Compassion: Treating Yourself with Kindness

Self, compassion involves treating yourself with the same kindness, understanding, and patience you would offer to a friend in a similar situation. It's easy to fall into patterns of self, criticism or blame after a heartbreak, but self, compassion encourages a more nurturing and forgiving relationship with yourself.

Practicing self, compassion can include simple acts of self, care, such as resting, engaging in activities that bring you joy, or allowing yourself to feel your emotions without judgment. Mindfulness meditation focused on self, compassion can also be a powerful tool for healing, fostering a healthier relationship with your inner self.

8. Forgiveness: Letting Go of Resentment

Forgiveness, whether directed toward others or yourself, is a vital step in the healing process. Holding onto anger, resentment, or guilt can keep you trapped in emotional pain and negativity. Forgiveness is not about justifying harmful behavior or forgetting what happened; rather, it's about freeing yourself from the weight of negative emotions and thoughts.

The process of forgiveness can be challenging, but by letting go of resentment, you reclaim your emotional energy and focus on your healing journey.

9. Reframing the Narrative: Finding Meaning in Pain

One of the most powerful techniques for emotional healing is reframing your experience to find meaning or lessons in the pain. This doesn't mean minimizing the hurt, but rather looking for ways in which the experience has contributed to your personal growth or deeper understanding.

Reframing helps shift your perspective from victimhood to empowerment, where you see yourself as an active participant in your healing rather than a passive recipient of pain. It can foster resilience and hope, reminding you that even in the midst of suffering, there is potential for growth and transformation.

Healing is not about erasing pain, but about integrating it into your life in a way that allows you to move forward with strength, understanding, and confidence. Each technique offers a different pathway to healing, and by exploring them, you can find the ones that resonate most with your unique experience and needs.

Building a Support System

Building a support system is an essential part of emotional healing, especially when dealing with a broken heart. While healing is a personal journey, having a network of supportive people around you can significantly enhance both the pace and depth of your recovery. A strong support system provides comfort, encouragement, and perspective, helping you navigate the emotional challenges that arise during difficult times.

1. **Identifying Your Support Needs**

    The first step in building a support system is understanding your specific emotional needs. These can vary greatly depending on your personality, the nature of your pain, and your coping mechanisms. Some people may need constant reassurance and frequent conversations, while others might prefer occasional check, ins and more reserved forms of support. Reflecting on what you truly need at this moment, whether it's someone to listen without judgment, offer practical advice, or simply distract you with enjoyable activities, will help you better communicate these needs to those around you.

2. Diversifying Your Support Network

It's important to recognize that no single person can fulfill all your emotional needs. Therefore, diversifying your support network is essential. This might include friends, family, colleagues, and even professional counselors or therapists. Each person in your network can offer different types of support. For instance, a close friend might be your go, to person for emotional venting, while a mentor or counselor could help you gain perspective and promote personal growth. Including different types of relationships in your support system ensures that you have access to the right kind of help when you need it.

3. Establishing Open Communication

For your support system to be effective, clear and honest communication is fundamental. Let the people in your support network know what you are going through and how they can best help you. It's also essential to set boundaries and be honest about what you need and what might be overwhelming for you. For example, you might need space and not be ready to discuss certain aspects of your situation. Clearly communicating these needs helps prevent misunderstandings and ensures that your support system works in a truly beneficial way for you.

4. Seeking Professional Support

While friends and family are invaluable, professional support can provide an additional level of care that might be necessary during emotionally difficult times. Therapists, counselors, and support groups offer a safe and structured environment to explore your emotions in depth. They can also introduce you to coping strategies and tools specifically designed to facilitate emotional healing. If you are dealing with complex emotions or past traumas, professional help can be particularly beneficial in guiding you toward a deeper and more lasting recovery.

5. Being Open to Receiving Help

Building a support system isn't just about identifying and reaching out to others; it's also about being open to receiving help with humility and honesty. Many people struggle with accepting support, feeling that they need to handle everything on their own. However, allowing yourself to rely on others during difficult times is a sign of strength, not weakness. Embrace the help offered by your support network, and remember that healing is a journey best undertaken with the assistance of those who care about you.

By identifying your needs, diversifying your support network, communicating openly, seeking professional help, and being open to receiving assistance, you can create a robust support system that aids your emotional recovery and contributes to your overall well, being.

Chapter 8:
Forgiveness and Letting Go

Forgiveness and letting go are two of the most challenging yet liberating actions you can take on the path to emotional serenity. This chapter explores the profound impact that forgiveness and letting go have on our mental, emotional, and even physical well, being, highlighting their essential role in overcoming past wounds, traumas, and disappointments.

Forgiveness is often misunderstood. Many people believe that forgiving someone means justifying their actions or forgetting the harm they caused. However, forgiveness is not about excusing behavior or pretending nothing happened; it's about freeing yourself from the emotional burden of holding onto resentment, anger, or pain. It is an act of self, love, where you choose to release the hold that the past has on you, allowing you to move forward with your life.

In practice, forgiveness is a conscious decision to let go of the negative emotions associated with a person or event. This doesn't mean that the pain disappears instantly, but it marks the beginning of a healing process where the emotional weight gradually lightens. We will explore various perspectives on forgiveness, including the benefits it brings not only to emotional health but also to physical well, being. Scientific studies have shown that those who practice forgiveness tend to experience lower stress levels, reduced blood pressure, and a stronger immune system. The mind, body connection is powerful, and self, forgiveness plays a key role in improving overall health.

Letting go is closely related to forgiveness, but it focuses more on releasing attachment to outcomes, people, or situations that no longer serve you. It involves accepting that some things are beyond our control and choosing to move forward without carrying the emotional baggage of the past. Letting go requires a form of surrender, recognizing that clinging to past hurts or unmet expectations only prolongs suffering. It's about reclaiming your energy and redirecting it toward more positive and constructive purposes.

One of the biggest challenges of letting go is the fear of the unknown. Holding onto the past, even when it's painful, can provide a sense of familiarity and control. Letting go requires trust, trust in yourself, trust in the process of life, and trust that the future holds opportunities for growth, joy, and fulfillment. This chapter will guide you through the steps of letting go, offering practical advice on how to free yourself from the past and open up to the possibilities of the present and future.

We will also address the importance of self, forgiveness. Often, the most difficult person to forgive is ourselves. Whether it's for mistakes made, missed opportunities, or perceived failures, self, forgiveness is crucial for inner peace. Holding onto guilt or shame can be as damaging as harboring resentment toward others. We will explore techniques to cultivate self, forgiveness, helping you break free from the cycle of self, blame and embrace a more compassionate and understanding relationship with yourself.

Forgiveness and letting go are not one, time events but ongoing practices that can be integrated into daily life. They are powerful tools that allow you to reclaim your personal power, live in harmony with your values, and create a life defined not by the pain of the past, but by the possibilities of the present.

Forgiving Yourself and Others

Forgiveness, whether directed toward yourself or others, is one of the most profound acts of healing you can undertake for your personal growth. It is a crucial step in releasing the past and moving forward with clarity and peace. Although it may seem simple in theory, practicing forgiveness can be incredibly challenging, especially when the wounds run deep. However, by approaching forgiveness with empathy and understanding, both toward yourself and others, you can begin to free yourself from the emotional burdens that hold you back.

Forgiving Yourself

Forgiving yourself is often the most difficult part of the process because we tend to be our own harshest critics, clinging to guilt, shame, and regret long after others have forgiven us or even after the situation has passed. This self, criticism can create a toxic cycle of negative thoughts that prevent you from moving forward and fully experiencing joy.

To start the journey of self, forgiveness, it is essential first to recognize and accept your humanity. Everyone makes mistakes; it's part of being human. Acknowledge that your mistakes do not define you and that you are not alone in having moments of weakness or poor judgment. Forgiving yourself means seeing yourself with compassion and understanding, rather than through the lens of harsh judgment, which ultimately hinders your growth.

Treat yourself with the same kindness and empathy you would offer a dear friend. If a friend came to you burdened with guilt or regret, what would you say? Most likely, you would comfort them, remind them of their worth, and encourage them to learn from their experiences rather than dwelling on them. Try to offer yourself that same level of compassion.

Another important aspect of self, forgiveness is recognizing the lessons learned from your mistakes. Instead of focusing on the error itself, shift your attention to what you gained from the experience. Did it teach you something valuable? Did it make you stronger or more resilient? By reframing the situation, you can transform a source of pain into an opportunity for growth. Remember, we grew up making mistakes, like when we first learned to walk or ride a bike; we fell, got hurt, but today we can walk, run, and ride with confidence!

Forgiving Others

Forgiving others, especially when they have caused deep wounds or betrayal, can seem like an impossible task, particularly in the early stages. However, holding onto resentment and anger only perpetuates the pain, keeping you emotionally tied to the past. Forgiveness is not about excusing others' actions or forgetting what happened; it's about freeing yourself from the negative emotions that hold you back and poison your emotional well, being.

The first step in forgiving others is acknowledging the pain that was caused. Allow yourself to feel the hurt, anger, or sadness without judgment. These emotions are important and deserve to be recognized, but once you have acknowledged them, it is essential not to dwell on them because holding onto anger or resentment can create a cycle of negativity that impacts your overall well, being.

Forgiveness also involves understanding the other person's perspective. This doesn't mean you have to agree with their actions, but trying to see the situation from their point of view can help you develop empathy and compassion. Often, people hurt others because they themselves are hurting. Recognizing this can help you begin to let go of anger and replace it with a sense of understanding.

Finally, it is important to remember that forgiveness is a process, not a one, time event. It may take time to fully let go of the pain and resentment, and that's okay. Be patient with yourself as you work through these emotions, and remember that every step toward forgiveness is a step toward healing and personal growth.

The Power of Forgiveness

Forgiving yourself and others does not mean being weak or giving in. On the contrary, forgiveness is a powerful act of strength and courage. It allows you to reclaim your power, free yourself from the past, and open yourself up to the possibilities of the future. By embracing forgiveness, you can create space for love, joy, and peace in your life and move forward with a lighter heart.

Remember, forgiveness is a gift you give to yourself. It's about letting go of the past and choosing to live in the present with grace, faith, and compassion. It's a journey that requires patience, but the benefits are immeasurable. As you continue on your path to forgiveness, know that you are not alone; many have walked this path before you, and many will walk it after you. And with each step, you move closer to a life filled with peace, happiness, and emotional freedom.

The Process of Letting Go

Letting go is a complex and deeply personal journey that is essential for emotional healing and personal growth. While it's often easier said than done, learning how to release the pain of the past, unmet expectations, or persistent attachments is fundamental to moving forward in life with a sense of peace and clarity. This process is not about forgetting or diminishing the importance of your experiences; rather, it's about freeing yourself from the hold these experiences have on you, allowing you to live more fully in the present and embrace the possibilities of the future.

1. Recognizing the Need to Let Go

The first step in letting go is recognizing when and why it's necessary. Often, we hold on to people, situations, or emotions because they feel familiar, even when we know they cause pain. It's crucial to identify what is no longer serving you, whether it's a relationship that has run its course, a past mistake that you keep replaying, or an expectation that prevents you from accepting reality. This awareness is the foundation for change, as it allows you to consciously decide to release what is holding you back.

Recognizing the need to let go requires complete honesty with yourself and a willingness to confront uncomfortable truths. It might involve acknowledging that a relationship is toxic or that a particular goal is no longer aligned with who you are today. This step is not about judging yourself or others but about creating the space to move forward.

2. Accepting Your Emotions

Letting go doesn't mean suppressing or ignoring your emotions. Instead, it involves fully experiencing and acknowledging your feelings before you can release them. Whether you feel sadness, anger, disappointment, or regret, these emotions are natural responses to loss and change. Allow yourself to feel them without judgment, understanding that they are part of the healing process.

It's important to give yourself time to grieve what you are letting go of. Grief is not limited to the loss of a loved one; it can also be a response to the end of a relationship, the realization of unmet expectations, or the need to abandon a long, held dream.

3. Detaching from the Outcome

One of the most challenging aspects of letting go is detaching from the outcome or expectations. Often, we hold on to people or situations because we are attached to a specific result or because we fear the unknown. Detaching from the outcome means releasing the need to control what happens next and trusting that, regardless of the result, you will be okay.

This step involves shifting your focus from external outcomes to inner peace. It's about recognizing that your worth and happiness are not dependent on a particular person, job, or achievement. By detaching from the outcome, you allow yourself to be open to new possibilities and experiences that might be even better than what you initially imagined.

4. Practicing Forgiveness

Forgiveness is a vital part of the letting go process. Whether it's forgiving someone else or forgiving yourself, holding on to resentment and anger keeps you tied to the past. You must free yourself from the emotional burden of holding a grudge.

Practicing forgiveness allows you to reclaim your emotional energy and focus on the present and future. It's a conscious decision to let go of the pain and anger associated with past events, which in turn enables you to move forward with a lighter heart.

5. **Embracing Change**

Letting go is, in essence, embracing change. It's about recognizing that life is in a constant state of flux and that holding on to the past prevents you from fully living in the present and future. Embracing change requires a shift in mindset from fear to acceptance, from clinging to releasing.

Change can be frightening because it involves stepping into the unknown. However, it is also an opportunity for growth, learning, and new experiences. By embracing change, you allow yourself to evolve and adapt, which is essential for personal development.

6. Moving Forward with Intention

The final step in letting go is moving forward with intention. This means setting new goals, cultivating new habits, and focusing on what you want to create in your life. Moving forward with intention helps you channel your energy into positive and constructive actions rather than dwelling on the past.

As you move forward, it's important to be patient with yourself. Letting go is not a one, time event but a continuous practice. There may be moments when old feelings resurface or when you feel tempted to hold on again. In these moments, remind yourself of your intention to let go and trust the process.

The Rewards of Letting Go

The process of letting go is a transformative journey of self, discovery and personal growth. It's not just about releasing what no longer serves you but about opening the door to new possibilities that align with your true self. Recognizing the need to let go, accepting your emotions, detaching from specific outcomes, practicing forgiveness, cultivating mindfulness, and embracing change are all essential steps in creating a space for growth and renewal.

Imagine the freedom of living a life no longer burdened by the weight of the past, but instead filled with experiences that nourish your soul and lead you toward authentic and joyful fulfillment. It requires patience, self, compassion, and trust, but the rewards are extraordinary: a life lived with greater freedom, peace, and a deep sense of satisfaction that comes from knowing you are living in alignment with your true self.

By letting go, you not only free yourself but also allow yourself to flourish in ways you may have never imagined. Embark on this journey with an open heart, trusting that each step brings you closer to a life richer in meaning, joy, and serenity.

Exercise: Forgiveness Letter

Forgiveness is a crucial step toward emotional well-being, but it can be challenging to achieve. Writing a forgiveness letter is an effective way to express and confront the feelings that might be holding you back. This exercise will guide you through the steps of creating a forgiveness letter, which can be addressed to yourself or someone else. There's no need to send this letter; the goal is to use writing as a tool for reflection and healing.

Instructions:

1. **Find a Quiet Environment:** Before you start, find a place where you feel comfortable and won't be disturbed. If you like, you can light a candle or play some relaxing music in the background to create a calm atmosphere.

2. **Reflect on Who or What You Want to Forgive:** Take a moment to consider the person, situation, or yourself that you want to forgive. Acknowledge the emotions associated with this situation, anger, pain, disappointment, or sadness. Be completely honest with yourself about how you feel.

3. **Start Your Letter:**

    - **Opening:** Begin the letter with a simple greeting, such as "Dear [Name]" or "Dear Me."

    - **Express Your Emotions:** Write openly about how you feel regarding the situation or person. Don't hold back; let your thoughts and feelings flow freely. It's important to recognize and validate the pain you've experienced.

    - **Acknowledge the Pain:** Explain why the situation hurt you and how it has affected you. This step helps you process the pain and bring it to light.

4. **Move Toward Forgiveness:**

    - **Express Forgiveness:** When you're ready, write your intention to forgive. You might say something like, "I choose to forgive you for..." or "I forgive myself for..."

    - **Release the Emotional Weight:** Express your willingness to release the emotional burden you've been carrying. This is an act of liberation for yourself.

5. **Close the Letter:**

    - **Positive Affirmation:** End the letter with a positive affirmation that reflects your desire to move forward, such as "I deserve peace and serenity, " or "I choose to create space for healing in my life."

    - **Signature:** Sign the letter as a symbol of completing the process.

6. **Decide What to Do with the Letter:** Once finished, you can choose to keep the letter in a safe place, destroy it as a symbolic act of release, or even burn it. The point is to do what feels most liberating and meaningful to you.

This exercise is a powerful way to confront and release repressed emotions. Writing a forgiveness letter is not just an act of healing but a gift you give to yourself to free yourself from the burden of the past. Review the letter in the future if you feel the need, and remember that forgiveness is a continuous process, not a one, time event.

Chapter 9:
Building Self, Esteem

Solid self, esteem is the cornerstone of personal growth and emotional well, being. It's not just about how we perceive ourselves; it shapes how we interact with the world around us. Self, esteem is the foundation upon which we build our lives, influencing every aspect of our relationships, work, and even mental and physical health.

Often, low self, esteem is a result of negative experiences, constant criticism, or harmful messages received throughout our lives. This can manifest as negative self, talk, fear of failure, or a constant feeling of not being enough. These emotions can limit our potential and prevent us from living the fulfilling life we deserve.

In this chapter, we'll explore how to reshape self, esteem, moving from a critical self, view to a genuine appreciation of our qualities and potential. Naturally, this transformation doesn't happen overnight; it requires ongoing commitment and a willingness to confront and change self, destructive thoughts and behaviors. We'll discuss how to develop greater self, awareness, improve self, image, and recognize our intrinsic worth, regardless of external judgments or circumstances.

A key aspect of building self, esteem is learning to treat ourselves with the same kindness and understanding that we offer to others, or even more so! It's about cultivating self, compassion, a topic we've touched on before but will explore more deeply here. Being kind to ourselves, especially during times of difficulty or failure, can transform how we see ourselves and open us up to genuine love and care for our well, being.

This chapter will not only provide insights and strategies but also include practical exercises to apply what you learn. Through positive affirmations, recognizing your successes, and working on your inner self, image, you can begin to build a solid foundation of self, esteem. Remember that the journey to building self, esteem is unique for each of us, and every small step forward is a success to be acknowledged and celebrated.

The ultimate goal is to empower you to live with greater confidence, make decisions that reflect your true desires and values, and develop healthier, more fulfilling relationships. Building self, esteem is an act of love toward yourself that can profoundly transform your life, paving the way for greater happiness, fulfillment, and inner peace.

Steps to Improve Self, Worth

Enhancing and strengthening self, esteem is a gradual process that involves commitment, self, awareness, and a desire to change how you view yourself. This journey is built day by day, through small actions and choices that, over time, can lead to meaningful transformation.

Below are some concrete steps you can take to nurture your self, worth and build a healthy sense of self, esteem:

1. **Practice Self, Awareness** The first step in improving self, esteem is becoming aware of your thoughts and internal dialogue. This means learning to "listen" to yourself. Often, low self, esteem is fueled by negative thoughts that play repeatedly in your mind, often rooted in past experiences or upbringing. Notice how you speak to yourself. Are you overly critical? Do you downplay your achievements? Being aware of these thought patterns is the first step in changing them. Start by noting these thoughts and replacing them with positive, realistic affirmations. For example, instead of thinking, *"I'm not good enough,"* try saying, *"I'm doing my best and getting better every day!"*

2. **Celebrate Your Successes, Even the Small Ones** We often overlook our successes and focus only on what we think we haven't done well. Learn to celebrate your achievements, no matter how small they may seem. Keep a success journal where you jot down daily accomplishments, no matter how minor. This practice helps shift your focus to what you are doing right and acknowledges your worth. Celebrating your successes reinforces your self, esteem and fosters a more positive self, image.

3. **Surround Yourself with Positive and Supportive People** The people around us significantly influence our sense of self, worth. Make an effort to be around positive individuals who support, respect, and believe in you. Limit interactions with those who are critical or dismissive. Healthy, supportive relationships act as a mirror, reflecting a positive image of yourself and helping to maintain strong self, esteem. Set boundaries with those who don't respect your emotional needs, and remember to prioritize your well, being.

4. **Take Care of Yourself** How you treat yourself physically reflects how you feel about yourself internally. Self, care is a tangible demonstration of love and respect for yourself. This includes eating well, exercising regularly, getting enough sleep, and engaging in activities that bring you joy. Small acts of self, care, such as enjoying a relaxing bath or pursuing a hobby, can greatly enhance your sense of well, being and self, esteem.

5. **Make Peace with Your Past** Past experiences can impact our self, esteem. It's crucial to confront and make peace with the past to build a more positive future. This might mean forgiving yourself for past mistakes, accepting painful experiences, or letting go of old resentments (as discussed in Chapter 6). If the past continues to weigh heavily on you, consider seeking the help of a therapist. Making peace with your past frees you to live more authentically and confidently in the present.

6. **Develop Skills and Competencies** Investing in your personal development can significantly boost your self, esteem. Learn something new, take a course, develop a hobby, or cultivate a talent. In today's world, there are countless online opportunities for growth. Gaining new skills and knowledge not only enhances your self, esteem but also provides a sense of accomplishment and satisfaction. Feeling competent in something allows you to see your value, recognize your abilities, and focus on personal goals rather than past hurts.

7. **Practice Gratitude** Gratitude is a powerful tool for improving self, esteem. Focusing on what you have, rather than what you lack, helps you view your life in a more positive light. Each day, take a few minutes to reflect on three things you're grateful for. This simple act can change your perspective and bring more joy into your life.

Improving self, esteem is a continuous journey that requires patience and dedication, but every step you take brings you closer to the most authentic and fulfilling version of yourself. Remember that every effort, no matter how small, is an investment in your emotional well, being and personal growth. You are worthy of love, respect, and a life filled with joy and fulfillment. Embrace this journey with enthusiasm and openness, knowing that you are building a solid foundation for a future full of confidence, satisfaction, and serenity. Believe in it because you truly deserve the best!

Overcoming Negative Self, Talk

Negative self, talk can act like a persistent background noise, eroding our self, esteem and limiting our potential. It's that internal voice that questions our abilities, criticizes our mistakes, and undermines our successes. This type of inner dialogue can be damaging, contributing to anxiety, depression, and feelings of inadequacy. Learning to transform this negative self, talk into positive and constructive thoughts is essential for improving self, esteem and living a more peaceful and fulfilling life.

Below are some effective strategies to help recognize and transform negative self, talk:

1. **Recognize and Identify Negative Self, Talk**

   The first step to overcoming negative self, talk is becoming aware of it. Often, these thoughts are so automatic that we don't realize how frequently they occur. Start by paying attention to your internal dialogue, especially in challenging situations. Notice the critical phrases that come up, such as, "I'm not good enough" or "I'm definitely going to fail." Becoming aware of these patterns is crucial for beginning the process of change. Awareness is the foundation of transformation.

2. **Challenge Your Negative Thoughts**

Once you've identified negative thoughts, the next step is to challenge them. Don't accept these thoughts as facts. Ask yourself, "Is there solid evidence supporting this thought?" Often, negative thoughts are exaggerations or distortions of reality. It can be helpful to write down these thoughts and respond to each one with a more balanced perspective. For instance, if you find yourself thinking, "I never do anything right," you could counter with, "There are many things I've done well before, and I can do them well again."

3. **Replace Negative Self, Talk with Positive Affirmations**

Positive affirmations can be a powerful tool in counteracting negative self, talk. Create affirmations that are encouraging and empowering, such as, "I am capable and worthy of success," or "Every day, I'm getting closer to my goals." Repeat these affirmations whenever negative thoughts arise. The goal isn't to deceive yourself but to reshape your internal dialogue in a more supportive and realistic way. Remember, you have the power to choose your thoughts and focus!

4. **Cultivate Self, Compassion**

   Being kind to yourself is essential in overcoming negative self, talk. We are often far more critical of ourselves than we are of others. When you make a mistake, speak to yourself as you would to a friend facing the same situation. Instead of criticizing, offer words of encouragement and understanding. Remember, everyone makes mistakes, and each failure is an opportunity for growth.

5. **Practice Gratitude**

   Gratitude can counteract negative self, talk by shifting your focus from what you lack to what you have. Reflecting on what you're grateful for daily can help you maintain a more positive outlook and distance yourself from critical thoughts. Each day, think about three things you're grateful for and reflect on them. This practice can help you stay grounded and find joy in small moments, reducing the impact of negative thoughts.

6. **Create a Supportive Environment**

   Your environment significantly influences your self, talk. Surround yourself with people who are positive and supportive. Limit your exposure to those who are overly critical or negative. A positive environment helps nurture a healthier, more constructive internal dialogue, strengthening your self, esteem and well, being.

7. **Remember That Change Takes Time**

   Changing your self, talk doesn't happen overnight. It's an ongoing process that requires patience and practice. Every time you recognize a negative thought and replace it with a positive one, you're making progress. Keep working on it, knowing that every small step brings you closer to a more peaceful and joyful life.

Overcoming negative self, talk is a transformative process that can profoundly impact your self, esteem and overall emotional well, being. With persistence and dedication, you can cultivate a more supportive and loving inner dialogue, paving the way for a life filled with greater self, confidence and fulfillment.

Exercise:
Daily Positive Affirmations

Positive affirmations are a powerful tool for boosting self, esteem and transforming how we perceive ourselves and the world. This exercise is designed to help you incorporate affirmations into your daily routine, gradually shifting your inner dialogue to create a more constructive mindset. Remember, affirmations aren't just about repeating words; they're about retraining your mind to focus on what is positive and achievable.

Instructions:

1. **Choose Your Affirmations:**

    Start by selecting a few affirmations that resonate with you. These should be statements that inspire you and reflect your goals or values. Here are some examples to get you started:

    - "I deserve love and respect."
    - "I am capable of overcoming any challenge."
    - "Every day, I move closer to my goals."

- "I am grateful for the opportunities to grow and learn." You can also create personalized affirmations that are specific to your desires or aspirations. The key is that they are positive, present, focused, and empowering.

2. **Repeat Them Daily:**

Set aside time each day to repeat your affirmations, whether mentally, out loud, or by writing them in a journal. Consider doing this first thing in the morning, while looking in the mirror, or before bedtime. The aim is to find a quiet moment to focus on yourself without distractions. Visualize yourself embodying these affirmations as if they are already true. Engage fully in this practice to make it feel natural and genuine.

3. **Be Aware of Your Thoughts:**

Throughout your day, pay attention to any negative or self, critical thoughts. When you notice one, pause and replace it with a positive affirmation. For instance, if you catch yourself thinking, "I can't do this," try replacing it with, "I am strong and capable of achieving my goals." This practice helps reframe your mindset, gradually reducing the influence of negative thinking.

4. **Write Down Your Affirmations:**

   Keep a journal dedicated to your affirmations. Write them down daily, focusing on the most meaningful ones. This reinforces your positive intentions and gives you a tangible record to revisit during difficult times. Writing your affirmations helps reinforce them in your subconscious, enhancing their impact.

5. **Create a Positive Environment:**

   Place your affirmations in visible locations, such as on your bathroom mirror, desk, or refrigerator. This way, even when you're not actively repeating them, you'll be surrounded by positive reminders that support your emotional well, being.

6. **Persist and Be Patient:**

   As with any change, transforming your inner dialogue takes time and persistence. Initially, affirmations might feel awkward or unnatural, but continue practicing. Over time, they will become a natural part of your thinking process. Don't get discouraged if you don't see immediate changes, each repetition is a step toward stronger self, esteem and a more positive outlook.

By integrating these affirmations into your daily life, you can foster a more encouraging and empowering inner dialogue, leading to greater self, confidence and a sense of fulfillment.

Chapter 10:
Self, Reflection and Growth

Self, reflection is a vital component of personal growth and development. It involves taking a step back to examine your thoughts, emotions, and behaviors, gaining insight into how they shape your life. Through this process, you develop a deeper understanding of your patterns, beliefs, and motivations, empowering you to make intentional changes that foster a more fulfilling and purposeful life.

In this chapter, we will explore the significance of self, reflection as a tool for personal growth. Whether you are facing challenges, trying to understand your emotional responses, or seeking to improve your relationships, self, reflection provides the clarity needed to make informed and mindful choices. It encourages you to ask difficult questions, confront fears and insecurities, and acknowledge your strengths and accomplishments.

Self, reflection is not about self, judgment or criticism; it is about observing your experiences with compassion, curiosity, and a commitment to growth. It means taking the time to pause, step back, and view your life from a broader perspective. This practice helps you identify the areas where you are thriving and those that may need more attention or adjustment.

We will delve into various techniques and exercises that facilitate self, reflection. From journaling and meditation to creating personal growth maps, these tools are designed to help you connect with your inner self, set meaningful goals, and monitor your progress. By dedicating time to regular and genuine self, reflection, you can cultivate a deeper understanding of yourself, enhance your emotional resilience, and set the stage for continuous development.

Remember, personal growth is a lifelong journey, not a destination. Each step toward greater self, awareness brings you closer to living a life aligned with your true values and aspirations. By embracing the practice of self, reflection, you choose to live with intention, mindfulness, and a commitment to becoming the best version of yourself.

The Importance of Self, Reflection

Self, reflection is a powerful tool for personal growth and emotional development. In our fast, paced world, filled with constant distractions and commitments, taking the time to pause and reflect can seem like a luxury. Yet, it is precisely in these moments of introspection that we find answers to deeper questions about ourselves, our lives, and our future direction.

Self, reflection allows us to step back from the busyness of daily life and observe what we are experiencing and how we are managing it. Through this process, we can explore our thoughts, feelings, and behaviors, gaining a better understanding of what drives us, what concerns us, and what brings us joy. This awareness is essential, as it enables us to live more authentically and intentionally, aligning our actions with our true values and goals.

A crucial aspect of self, reflection is the ability to examine our emotions and reactions. Often, when faced with stressful or conflicting situations, we respond automatically, without fully understanding why. Self, reflection gives us the space to ask ourselves, "Why did I react that way?" or "What emotions influenced my behavior in that moment?" By asking these questions, we can identify our defense mechanisms, uncover hidden fears, and work on developing greater emotional resilience.

For example, if we notice that we respond with anger or frustration when we feel criticized, we can explore where this reaction comes from. It might stem from past insecurities or a need for self, protection. Recognizing these patterns allows us to find more constructive ways of responding to criticism and managing our emotions.

Self, reflection is not only about identifying areas for improvement but also about acknowledging our achievements and strengths. We often focus so much on what is lacking that we forget to appreciate what we have accomplished. Taking the time to reflect on our successes, no matter how small, helps us build a more positive self, image and strengthens our self, esteem. For instance, we can ask ourselves, "What positive things have I done this week?" or "What challenges have I recently overcome?" Celebrating these victories gives us the motivation and confidence to face future challenges with a more optimistic mindset.

In addition to recognizing our successes, self, reflection helps us pinpoint areas where we want to grow. This is not about judging ourselves harshly, but about honestly assessing aspects of our lives that could benefit from change. For instance, we might notice that we tend to procrastinate or avoid situations that make us uncomfortable. Acknowledging these behaviors is the first step towards positive change. We can then ask ourselves, "What concrete steps can I take to improve in this area?" and set specific, achievable goals for personal development.

Self, reflection becomes truly impactful when we ask ourselves meaningful questions that go beyond the surface. Questions like "What truly makes me happy?" or "What values guide my decisions?" prompt us to delve deeply into who we are and what we want from life. Immediate answers are not necessary; what matters is maintaining an open and curious mindset, willing to explore and learn continually.

To gain the most from self, reflection, it is helpful to create a dedicated space for this practice. This could be a physical space, like a quiet corner of your home where you can sit undisturbed, or a designated time of day when you can engage in self, reflection. Activities like journaling, meditation, or simply sitting quietly and contemplating can become daily rituals that help you stay connected to your inner self.

It is also important to approach self, reflection with compassion. It is easy to fall into the trap of self, criticism, but this does not lead to genuine growth. Instead, approach yourself with kindness and understanding, recognizing that every mistake is an opportunity for learning and that personal growth is an ongoing journey. When we acknowledge our limitations and accept our imperfections, we open ourselves to the possibility of authentic and lasting change.

The practice of self, reflection not only enhances self, understanding but also builds resilience. Being aware of our thoughts and emotions helps us face challenges with greater balance and respond more consciously and thoughtfully. This emotional resilience strengthens our ability to handle difficulties, recover after setbacks, and discover the opportunities hidden within adversity.

In conclusion, self, reflection is a powerful tool for creating a life that resonates with who we truly are. By taking the time to look inward, we can uncover hidden aspects of our personality, approach challenges with greater wisdom, and build a future that reflects our values and aspirations. Every moment of reflection is a step toward greater self, awareness and a more authentic version of ourselves. Remember, personal growth is not a one, time event but a continuous process of exploration, learning, and transformation. Embrace this journey with an open heart and a curious mind, knowing that each step brings you closer to the best version of yourself.

Exercise:
Creating a Personal Growth Map

Creating a personal growth map is an effective way to visualize your development path and stay focused on your self, improvement goals. This tool allows you to see where you currently are, where you want to go, and what steps you need to take to get there. It serves as a practical, visual guide that helps you navigate your journey of personal growth, keeping your motivation high and reminding you of your aspirations.

Step 1: Define Areas of Growth

>Start by identifying the areas of your life where you want to improve. These could include aspects like career, physical health, emotional development, relationships, or mental well, being. Take a moment to reflect on which areas of your life need more attention. Ask yourself: **In which areas do I feel unsatisfied? Where do I see the most potential for growth?**

Step 2: Set Clear and Specific Goals

Once you have identified the areas for growth, set clear and specific goals for each one. Make sure these goals are both motivating and achievable. This is where the "SMART" method comes into play, helping you create goals that are *Specific, Measurable, Achievable, Relevant,* and *Time, bound.* For example, instead of setting a vague goal like "I want to be healthier," specify it as, "I will exercise for 30 minutes, five times a week." This way, your goals are more concrete and easier to follow.

Step 3: Create a Detailed Action Plan

After establishing your goals, it's essential to create a detailed action plan. This plan should include the specific steps you intend to take to achieve each goal. For instance, if one of your goals is to improve your communication skills, your action plan might include enrolling in a public speaking course, practicing in social settings, or reading books on effective communication. Make sure to break your goals into smaller, manageable steps to avoid feeling overwhelmed.

Step 4: Visualize Your Path

Now that you've set your goals and outlined your action steps, it's time to visualize your path. Use a large sheet of paper, a whiteboard, or mind, mapping software to create a visual representation of your personal growth map. Place your main goals in the center and draw lines connecting each goal to the related action steps. Use different colors to represent different areas of your life, such as health, work, relationships, and personal development. This visualization will help you see the bigger picture and stay focused on your goals.

Step 5: Monitor and Reevaluate Regularly

Your map should not be a static document. Review it regularly, at least once a month, to assess your progress and evaluate where you stand. Ask yourself: **Am I on the right track to achieve my goals? Are there any obstacles I didn't anticipate? Is there something I can do differently to improve my results?** Be open to adjusting your goals and action plans based on your progress and any new insights you gain.

Step 6: Celebrate Your Successes

Acknowledging and celebrating your successes is a crucial part of the personal growth process. Every time you reach a goal or surpass a milestone, take a moment to recognize your efforts. This celebration can be as simple as treating yourself to something special or taking a day to relax and reflect. Celebrating your progress helps reinforce positive behavior and keeps you motivated to continue working towards your goals.

Step 7: Use the Map as a Daily Guide

Your personal growth map should serve as a daily guide to remind you of your priorities and keep you focused. Place it somewhere visible, such as on your desk or workspace, so you have a constant visual reminder of your goals. Whenever you feel stuck or discouraged, refer to your map to regain your direction and remind yourself why you chose this path of growth.

Following these steps will turn your personal growth map into a powerful, ongoing tool. It will keep you focused, motivated, and resilient, helping you stay on track and steadily work towards becoming the best version of yourself.

Chapter 11:
Establishing Healthy Boundaries

Establishing healthy boundaries is a fundamental element of personal growth and emotional well, being. Boundaries are not barriers we build to exclude others, but guidelines we establish to protect our personal space and uphold our values. They enable us to communicate clearly what is acceptable and what is not, fostering more balanced and respectful relationships with both ourselves and others.

In a world where we are constantly exposed to external pressures, setting boundaries helps us maintain our integrity and live more authentically. However, many people struggle to say "no" or set clear limits, often out of fear of disappointing others or appearing selfish. Yet, learning to define and respect our boundaries is essential for our mental and physical health, as well as for our overall satisfaction in life.

In this chapter, we will explore what it truly means to have healthy boundaries and how they can positively impact our lives. We will discuss how to recognize personal boundaries, how to communicate them effectively, and how to maintain them even in the face of external pressures. You will learn that establishing boundaries does not mean isolating yourself but rather creating a safe space where you can grow, connect with others in a genuine way, and honor your own needs and desires.

Remember, setting healthy boundaries is an act of love and respect toward yourself. It is a statement that you deserve to be treated with dignity and that your needs are just as important as those of others. By practicing this, you can cultivate stronger and more authentic relationships and live a life that truly reflects who you are and what you value.

Recognizing and Setting Boundaries

Recognizing and setting boundaries is one of the most valuable skills for achieving a balanced and fulfilling life. Boundaries are like invisible lines that define where we end and others begin. They act as personal guidelines that dictate how we want to be treated, what behaviors we find acceptable, and what we are willing to tolerate. These boundaries can apply to different aspects of our lives, such as time, emotions, physical space, and even mental and spiritual resources.

Recognizing Your Boundaries

The first step in establishing healthy boundaries is to identify what your boundaries are. This requires self, awareness and introspection. It's crucial to understand what makes you feel comfortable and what doesn't, which situations leave you feeling drained or resentful, and when you feel respected or violated. To start, you can ask yourself these key questions:

- What situations make me feel uncomfortable or taken advantage of?
- When do I feel resentment toward others?

- In what moments do I feel the need to say 'no'?

- What makes me feel respected and valued?

Answering these questions can help you identify your personal limits. Often, feelings of emotional discomfort, resentment, or stress are indicators that your boundaries have been crossed. Paying attention to these emotions can guide you in understanding which boundaries you need to establish.

Setting Clear Boundaries

Once you have recognized your boundaries, it's essential to communicate them clearly. This means being assertive and respectful when expressing your needs. Setting boundaries is not an act of selfishness; it's a form of self, care. It signifies that you have a right to be treated with respect and dignity. Here are some steps to set clear boundaries:

- **Be Specific:** When setting a boundary, clearly state what you will and will not accept. For example, instead of saying, "I don't like it when you're like that," you could say, "I don't appreciate it when you raise your voice at me. I would prefer if we talked calmly."

- **Use "I" Statements:** Using first, person statements such as "I feel" or "I need" helps you communicate your feelings and needs without sounding accusatory.

- **Be Consistent:** Once you have set your boundaries, it's important to maintain them consistently. Allowing others to disregard your boundaries without consequence sends mixed messages and can lead to further frustration.

- **Prepare for Reactions:** Not everyone will respond positively to your boundaries. Some may feel offended or rejected. Be prepared for these reactions and remember that setting boundaries is about respecting yourself, not controlling others.

Practicing Self, Compassion

Establishing boundaries, particularly if you haven't done so in the past, can be challenging and requires courage. You may feel guilty or selfish, but remember that taking care of yourself is essential. Practicing self, compassion means treating yourself with the same kindness and understanding you would offer a friend in a similar situation. Recognizing that everyone has the right to set limits to protect their well, being is a fundamental step toward building self, esteem.

Reevaluating and Adjusting Boundaries

Boundaries are not set in stone; they can evolve as you grow and as circumstances change. It's important to regularly review your boundaries to ensure they are still serving you effectively. If a boundary is no longer relevant, or if you realize you need to establish a new one, feel free to adjust accordingly. Flexibility is a natural part of maintaining healthy boundaries.

Reinforcing Boundaries with Actions

Setting boundaries is more than just verbal communication, it also requires action. This means being prepared to uphold your boundaries and enforce consequences when they are crossed. For example, if you have set a boundary around your personal time and someone continues to ignore it, you may need to be firm in refusing additional requests or removing yourself from situations that don't respect your limits. Consistency in your actions demonstrates to others that you take your boundaries seriously.

By recognizing and setting boundaries, you take an essential step toward protecting your well, being and building more balanced, fulfilling relationships. Boundaries allow you to interact with others in a way that is respectful and true to your needs and values, enabling you to live a life that aligns with who you are.

The Power of Saying No

Saying "no" is a crucial skill for maintaining emotional well, being and establishing healthy boundaries. For many people, saying no can feel uncomfortable or even impossible due to social pressures, the desire to please others, or the fear of conflict and rejection. However, learning to say no is essential for protecting your energy and resources and for focusing on what truly matters. Understanding the importance of this word can transform how you interact with the world and significantly improve the quality of your life.

Saying no is not about being selfish or rude; it's about prioritizing your well, being. When you constantly say yes to everyone and everything, you risk overwhelming yourself, leading to stress, burnout, and resentment. This can damage not only your mental and physical health but also your relationships, making you feel taken advantage of or undervalued. Saying no creates space in your life for activities, people, and projects that genuinely align with your values and goals.

Moreover, saying no is a form of self, respect. It acknowledges that your time, energy, and emotions are valuable and that you have the right to decide how to invest them. It helps you live more authentically, focusing on what you genuinely desire and need rather than what others expect of you. This self, respect and authenticity lead to increased self, esteem and a stronger sense of personal identity.

Overcoming the Fear of Saying No

One of the biggest challenges in saying no is the fear of disappointing others or being perceived as rude or uncaring. It's natural to want to be liked and to avoid conflict, but it's also crucial to recognize that your primary responsibility is to yourself. If you constantly put others' needs before your own, you risk losing touch with your own desires and well, being. This can lead to feelings of resentment, frustration, and emotional exhaustion.

To overcome the fear of saying no, it's helpful to reframe how you think about it. Saying no doesn't mean rejecting the person; it simply means prioritizing your well, being. By taking care of yourself first, you'll be in a better position to support and help others when you genuinely can. Most people will understand and respect your decision if it is communicated with honesty and respect.

How to Say No Effectively

Learning to say no firmly and kindly is a valuable skill. Here are some tips on how to do it effectively:

1. **Be Direct and Clear:** When you say no, be straightforward. Avoid vague responses like "maybe" or "I'll think about it" if you know your answer is no. Instead, state your decision clearly, for example, "Thank you for thinking of me, but I can't commit to that project."

2. **Offer a Brief Explanation (If Necessary):** You are not obligated to provide a detailed explanation for your decision, but a brief rationale can help the other person understand your perspective. For example, "I need to prioritize my personal projects right now" or "I'm focusing on my health and need to take time for myself."

3. **Use the Broken Record Technique:** If someone persists after you've said no, calmly repeat your response. You can vary the wording slightly, but keep the message consistent. This technique reinforces your decision and shows that you are firm in your boundaries.

4. **Express Gratitude:** Acknowledge the request and express appreciation. Saying something like, "I really appreciate that you thought of me for this" shows that you value the relationship, even if you're declining the offer.

5. **Practice Saying No:** If you're not used to saying no, it can feel challenging at first. Start by practicing in low, stakes situations to build your confidence. Over time, it will become more natural to assert your boundaries.

The Benefits of Saying No

The act of saying no is incredibly empowering. It allows you to take control of your life, making conscious choices about how to invest your time and energy. This sense of control can lead to greater fulfillment as you focus on what truly matters to you. Additionally, saying no can improve your relationships. By establishing clear boundaries, you encourage mutual respect and understanding. People who respect your no are more likely to appreciate your yes, knowing it is given sincerely and without resentment.

Saying no also frees up time for self, care and personal growth. It allows you to invest in your health, hobbies, and passions, which ultimately make you a happier and more balanced person. This not only benefits you but also enhances your ability to contribute positively to the lives of others.

In conclusion, mastering the art of saying no is a powerful step towards living authentically and maintaining your emotional well, being. It's a skill that requires practice and courage, but the rewards are well worth the effort. By learning to say no with confidence and kindness, you create space for what truly matters in your life and build stronger, more genuine connections with others.

Exercise: Creating a Boundary List

Creating a personal boundary list is a practical and empowering exercise that helps you establish and maintain healthy boundaries in various areas of your life. This exercise encourages you to reflect deeply on what is acceptable to you and what is not, providing a clear framework that supports your emotional well, being and personal growth. By developing a boundary list, you can better manage your interactions with others, effectively organize your time and energy, and ensure that your needs are respected.

Step 1: Identify the Areas of Your Life That Need Boundaries

The first step is recognizing the areas of your life where boundaries are necessary. These might include relationships, work, personal time, social interactions, and emotional or mental space. Take some time to reflect on situations where you've felt overwhelmed, stressed, or taken advantage of. Ask yourself:

- When do I feel the most stressed?

- Are there people or situations that consistently make me feel uncomfortable?

- In what areas of my life do I feel my needs are being ignored?

These questions can help you pinpoint where boundaries are lacking and where new ones need to be established.

Step 2: Define Your Non, Negotiables

Once you've identified the areas that require boundaries, it's essential to define your non, negotiables, those fundamental principles you are not willing to compromise on. These can relate to your values, personal time, or specific ways you expect to be treated. For example:

- **Time:** "I need at least one hour a day for self, care without interruptions."

- **Respect:** "I will not tolerate being treated disrespectfully or being belittled."

- **Work, Life Balance:** "I don't check work emails after 7 PM or on weekends."

Having a list of non, negotiables helps you clearly articulate your limits and ensures that you remain firm on what matters most to you.

Step 3: Create a Boundary List

Now, begin drafting your boundary list based on the insights you've gained. Write down specific boundaries for each area of your life. Be as detailed as possible to avoid ambiguity about what you are willing to accept.

For example:

- **Personal Time:** "I will schedule at least one evening per week for my hobbies or relaxation, and I won't cancel these commitments unless there's an emergency."

- **Social Boundaries:** "I will not participate in conversations that I find overly negative. If a discussion becomes too toxic, I will gently remove myself."

- **Emotional Boundaries:** "I will not take on the responsibility for others' emotions. I can support friends and family, but I won't let their stress affect my mental health."

Step 4: Practice Communicating Your Boundaries

Establishing boundaries is one thing; communicating them effectively is another. Express your boundaries clearly and assertively without being confrontational. You might say:

- "I need some time to think about it; I'll get back to you later."

- "I really appreciate your invitation, but I need to rest tonight."

- "I feel uncomfortable when conversations become too gossipy. Can we talk about something else?"

Practicing these scenarios or writing them down can help you feel more comfortable when it comes time to communicate your boundaries in real, life situations.

Step 5: Regularly Review and Modify Your Boundary List

Your boundary list should be a dynamic document that evolves as your needs and circumstances change. Set aside time each month to review your list. Reflect on how well your boundaries are working and make adjustments as necessary. Ask yourself:

- Am I on the right track to achieving my goals?

- Are there new situations that require additional boundaries?

- Have some boundaries become less relevant over time?

Regularly updating your list will help keep it aligned with the current context of your life.

Step 6: Reinforce Boundaries with Actions

Developing a boundary list is effective only if you commit to reinforcing them through concrete actions. When someone crosses a boundary, respond appropriately by restating your limits or removing yourself from the situation if necessary. Consistency is key; the more you uphold your boundaries, the more others will respect them.

Step 7: Practice Self, Compassion

> Finally, remember that establishing and maintaining boundaries can be challenging, especially if it's a new practice for you. Be kind to yourself throughout this process. It's normal to feel guilty or uncomfortable initially, but these feelings will lessen over time as you become more accustomed to honoring your needs. Celebrate your progress and acknowledge the courage it takes to prioritize your well, being.

By developing and maintaining a boundary list, you empower yourself to live more authentically and in harmony with your values. This practice not only protects your emotional and mental health but also fosters healthier, more respectful relationships. As you continue to refine your boundaries, you'll find greater clarity, peace, and balance in your life.

Chapter 12:
Creating Healthy Relationships

Building healthy relationships is a crucial aspect of living a fulfilling and balanced life. Our connections with others profoundly influence our emotional well, being, personal growth, and overall happiness. Whether these relationships are with family members, friends, romantic partners, or coworkers, the quality of our interactions plays a significant role in shaping our experiences and perspectives. Healthy relationships offer support, joy, and a sense of belonging, while unhealthy ones can lead to stress, anxiety, and feelings of isolation.

In this chapter, we will explore the principles and practices that form the foundation for healthy, constructive relationships. It's important to understand that creating healthy relationships isn't just about finding the right people but also about becoming the right person. This involves self, awareness, empathy, communication, and a willingness to grow both individually and together with others.

Healthy relationships are built on mutual respect, trust, and understanding. They foster open communication, where each person feels safe to express their thoughts and feelings without fear of judgment or retaliation. In these relationships, boundaries are respected, and each person's needs are considered and valued. A healthy relationship thrives on balance, with both parties giving and receiving support, creating a dynamic of equality and collaboration.

Throughout this chapter, we will discuss the key elements for building and maintaining healthy relationships. We will analyze effective communication techniques that can enhance understanding and connection and explore the role of empathy in strengthening emotional bonds. Additionally, we will address strategies for managing conflict in ways that promote resolution and growth rather than resentment and distance.

It's essential to recognize that building healthy relationships starts with the relationship we have with ourselves. Self, love and self, respect form the foundation of how we interact with others. When we value ourselves, we are more likely to set and maintain boundaries, clearly express our needs, and engage in relationships that align with our values.

By understanding and applying these principles, you can cultivate relationships that are not only fulfilling but also contribute positively to your personal development. This journey requires patience, openness, and the courage to be vulnerable, but the rewards are immense: deeper connections, greater emotional security, and a support network that enriches your life. As we navigate this chapter, let's embrace the opportunity to grow together, build stronger relationships, and create a more compassionate and connected life.

Characteristics of Healthy Relationships

Healthy relationships are the cornerstone of a fulfilling and satisfying life. What sets a healthy relationship apart from an unhealthy one is not merely the absence of conflict, but the presence of fundamental traits that promote well, being, respect, and mutual growth. These relationships support us in times of need and enrich our daily lives by providing a sense of belonging and genuine connection.

Healthy relationships are characterized by a balanced dynamic in which both partners feel free to be themselves and express their needs and desires. It's not just about avoiding harmful or toxic behaviors but actively cultivating an environment of trust, respect, and mutual support. Communication is open and genuine, and conflicts are managed constructively, with the intention of understanding and resolving issues rather than dominating or winning.

- **Mutual Respect:** In a healthy relationship, each individual values the other for who they are, recognizing their limits and boundaries. This mutual respect not only strengthens trust but also promotes a sense of emotional security and stability.

- **Trust and Integrity:** Healthy relationships are built over time through consistent acts of honesty and reliability. Trust allows each person to feel secure and free to be vulnerable without fear of being judged or betrayed.

- **Authentic Communication:** A key characteristic of healthy relationships is the ability to communicate openly. This includes clear expression of feelings, active listening, and empathy to understand the other person's perspective.

- **Mutual Support:** In healthy relationships, individuals encourage and support each other. This support is not just emotional but can also translate into practical help, such as collaborating to achieve common goals or facing daily challenges together.

- **Fairness and Collaboration:** A fair balance between giving and receiving is essential for a healthy relationship. Both partners should feel valued and heard, contributing equally to the relationship, whether in decision, making or responsibilities.

- **Clear Boundaries:** Healthy relationships respect the need for personal space and individual boundaries. Recognizing and respecting these boundaries not only protects individuality but also strengthens mutual respect.

- **Constructive Conflict Management:** In healthy relationships, conflicts are seen as opportunities for growth and understanding, rather than threats. Differences are addressed with respect, seeking solutions that are satisfactory for both parties.

- **Shared Values and Common Goals:** Having similar values and goals helps to create a solid foundation for a relationship. When both partners share visions and aspirations, it's easier to work together to build a common future.

- **Authenticity and Freedom:** In a healthy relationship, both individuals feel free to be themselves, without the need to pretend or conform to what the other desires. This level of authenticity fosters a deep and genuine connection.

- **Joy and Positivity:** Healthy relationships bring happiness and joy. It's not about always agreeing or avoiding problems but about being able to find pleasure and satisfaction in the time spent together, valuing moments of joy and sharing.

In summary, healthy relationships are a combination of respect, trust, communication, and support. Cultivating these aspects not only enriches our personal lives but also helps us develop a network of meaningful connections that support and inspire us. By embracing these principles, we can build relationships that not only make us feel loved and valued but also encourage us to grow and improve as individuals.

Building Strong Connections

Strong connections not only help us feel less lonely but are also essential for our emotional and mental well, being. Building meaningful and lasting relationships requires intentionality and commitment. This process involves various qualities and actions that, when practiced consistently, can lead to deep and authentic bonds. Here are some key aspects to consider when building strong connections:

- **Active Listening and Engagement:** The first step in building strong connections is active listening. This goes beyond simply hearing the other person's words; it involves paying attention with your full mind and heart. This means putting aside distractions, maintaining eye contact, and showing genuine interest in what the other person is sharing. Asking open, ended questions and providing thoughtful feedback encourage deeper communication and demonstrate that we are present and engaged in the conversation.

- **Developing Empathy:** Empathy is the ability to understand and share the feelings of others. It is a fundamental component of strong connections because it allows us to approach others with genuine care and understanding. Showing empathy doesn't mean solving other people's problems, but being present with understanding and support. We can practice empathy by listening carefully, putting ourselves in the other person's shoes, and acknowledging their emotions without judgment.

- **Authenticity and Honesty:** The strongest relationships are built on truth and transparency. Being authentic means being open and honest about who we are, what we feel, and what we desire. This authenticity creates an environment where the other person also feels free to express themselves without fear of being judged. Honesty strengthens trust and promotes a deeper connection because both parties know they can rely on each other's integrity.

- **Being Vulnerable:** Being vulnerable means sharing our deepest thoughts, feelings, and fears. While vulnerability may seem risky, it is through it that the most meaningful connections are formed. When we are willing to show our weaknesses and insecurities, we allow others to see us for who we truly are. This openness fosters a sense of intimacy and mutual trust, demonstrating that we are human and trust the other person enough to be honest.

- **Dedication and Time:** Strong connections don't develop overnight; they require time and dedication. It is important to dedicate quality time to the people with whom we want to build a bond. This can include regular conversations, shared activities, or simply being available when the other person needs support. Consistency and presence are essential for strengthening bonds and showing that we care about the other person.

- **Mutual Support:** Strong relationships are based on a reciprocal exchange of support. This means being there for each other in times of need and knowing that we can rely on them when we need help. Mutual support is not just emotional; it can also include practical help, advice, or simply a listening ear. This exchange strengthens the sense of community and belonging.

- **Acknowledging and Celebrating Each Other's Successes:** Another key element in building strong connections is the ability to celebrate each other's successes and achievements. Showing joy and pride in the accomplishments of those we love strengthens the emotional bond and demonstrates that we genuinely care about their well, being and happiness. Acknowledging others' successes, rather than feeling envy or competition, creates an environment of positivity and mutual support.

- **Handling Conflicts Constructively:** Conflicts are a natural part of any relationship, but how they are managed can make the difference between a strong connection and a troubled relationship. It's important to approach conflicts with calmness, openness, and a willingness to find a solution that satisfies both parties. Avoiding blame and resentment, and instead focusing on understanding and resolution, helps overcome challenges without damaging the relationship.

In summary, building strong connections requires intentional effort and ongoing commitment. These connections not only enrich our lives but also provide a support system that helps us navigate difficulties and celebrate joys. By practicing active listening, empathy, authenticity, and mutual support, we can create relationships that are lasting, meaningful, and deeply satisfying.

Case Study:
Transforming Relationship Dynamics

Jessica and Michael met during their college years, and from the start, their relationship was filled with excitement and shared dreams. They were passionate about travel, loved exploring new cultures, and spent countless nights planning future adventures. After a few years of marriage, they settled in a small town where Jessica worked as an elementary school teacher, and Michael as a financial consultant. The early years of their marriage were filled with joy, and they maintained their shared passions by planning adventurous vacations and attending cultural events. Jessica managed most of the childcare while balancing work, and Michael focused on his career, often bringing work home. Their days were hectic, filled with early morning wake, ups, rushing to work, managing homework and extracurricular activities, and quick dinners before finally collapsing into bed.

As responsibilities grew, things began to change. Jessica decided to pursue a master's degree in education to advance her career, while Michael was promoted to a higher position that involved longer hours and frequent business trips. Within a few years, they had two children, Emily and Jacob, adding another layer of responsibility to their already busy lives. Conversations between Jessica and Michael became increasingly superficial, mostly about managing the household and the children, leaving little time for discussing their feelings, dreams, or fears. Jessica felt increasingly alone and overwhelmed by routine, lacking emotional support. Michael, on the other hand, felt constantly criticized, perceiving every conversation as a list of complaints. He felt inadequate as both a husband and a father and began withdrawing emotionally, turning to work or spending long evenings in front of the TV to avoid conflicts.

Tensions escalated when Jessica noticed that Michael often got distracted during their few conversations, responding to work messages even during family dinners. Arguments became more frequent and intense, often ending in silence and coldness. Both Jessica and Michael began to wonder if staying together was the right choice. Jessica felt trapped in a loveless marriage, while Michael felt unappreciated and unfulfilled. They even considered separating, thinking they might find greater happiness apart.

The Turning Point One evening, after another draining argument, Jessica confided in a close friend who had experienced a difficult divorce. The friend suggested trying couples therapy as a last effort to save the marriage. Though initially skeptical, Jessica proposed the idea to Michael, who, after some hesitation, agreed. Both realized they wanted to try to save their marriage, not only for the sake of their children but also because of the love they still felt for each other.

Steps Taken to Transform the Relationship

1. **Seeking Professional Help:** Jessica and Michael began attending weekly couples therapy sessions. They discovered that many of their issues stemmed from unspoken expectations and a lack of open communication. The therapist taught them techniques for more effective communication, such as active listening and using "I" statements to express their feelings without accusing each other. Jessica realized her criticism stemmed from feeling lonely and overwhelmed, while Michael understood his reluctance to talk was due to feeling inadequate and fearing he couldn't meet Jessica's expectations.

2. **Prioritizing Communication:** They decided to set aside one evening a week just for themselves. They would turn off their phones, put the kids to bed early, and spend time together without distractions. During these evenings, they focused on meaningful conversations, sharing thoughts, dreams, and concerns. This dedicated time allowed them to reconnect emotionally and rediscover the joy of sharing life with each other.

3. **Developing Empathy:** In therapy, Jessica and Michael began practicing empathy. Instead of reacting impulsively during conflicts, they learned to take a deep breath and try to understand each other's perspective. Jessica began to understand how work pressures affected Michael, while Michael recognized how challenging it was for Jessica to juggle work, the household, and the children almost single, handedly. This mutual empathy significantly reduced tensions and helped them collaborate more effectively.

4. **Reconnecting Through Shared Activities:** Remembering their love for travel, they decided to make time for short weekend getaways, even if just for a day trip. They also began planning a major vacation abroad, a dream they had set aside for years. Sharing new experiences and creating new memories helped them remember why they fell in love and brought them closer together.

5. **Balancing Work and Home Life:** Jessica and Michael worked together to rebalance their responsibilities. Jessica sought help from her family with the kids, giving her more time to focus on her work and personal well, being. Michael made a conscious effort to limit his work hours and fully disconnect when at home. By setting clearer boundaries between work and family, both found greater balance and peace of mind.

Outcome After months of effort, Jessica and Michael saw significant positive changes in their relationship. Arguments became less frequent and more constructive, focusing on problem, solving rather than venting frustrations. They felt a renewed connection and love for each other, similar to what they had experienced in the early years of their marriage. Their home became a place of safety and joy, and their children noticed and benefited from the positive change in their parents' behavior.

I share this story because it's close to my heart. I've had the privilege of witnessing the dedication and effort that Jessica and Michael put into transforming their relationship, and their journey has been truly inspiring. Their experience reaffirms my belief that with love, patience, and a genuine commitment to understanding one another, we can all create relationships that are not only strong and supportive but also deeply fulfilling and life, enhancing.

Chapter 13:
Emotional Balance and Mindfulness

Achieving emotional balance and practicing mindfulness are essential components of living a fulfilling and centered life. In today's fast, paced world, where distractions, responsibilities, and pressures are constant, it's all too easy to feel overwhelmed and disconnected from our inner selves. Emotional balance doesn't mean avoiding or suppressing our feelings; rather, it involves understanding and managing them in a healthy and constructive way. Mindfulness, on the other hand, helps us stay focused on the present, appreciate each moment with all its nuances, and develop greater awareness of our thoughts and emotions, allowing us to guide them more effectively.

This chapter will cover practical techniques and strategies for cultivating emotional balance and mindfulness in our daily lives. We will explore the importance of recognizing and accepting our emotions, understanding their origins, and finding constructive ways to respond to them. By doing so, we can prevent our emotions from controlling us, reduce stress, and enhance our overall well, being.

Mindfulness is a powerful tool that complements emotional balance by encouraging us to live in the present rather than getting trapped in worries about the past or future. Remember, the past is gone and cannot be changed, and the future is yet to come. It's crucial to fully savor the present moment. Through mindfulness practices, we can learn to observe our thoughts without judgment, develop greater self, awareness, and create space for inner peace. This chapter will introduce you to simple mindfulness exercises, such as deep breathing, meditation, and grounding techniques, which can be incorporated into even the busiest of schedules.

Together, emotional balance and mindfulness lay a solid foundation for resilience, clarity, and happiness. By embracing these practices, we empower ourselves to navigate the highs and lows of life with grace and stability, fostering a deeper connection with ourselves and those around us. As we delve into this chapter, let's open our hearts and minds to the possibility of living more intentionally, finding peace amidst chaos, and building a life rich in emotional health and mindfulness.

Techniques for Achieving Emotional Balance

Emotional balance is essential for leading a more peaceful and fulfilling life. It doesn't mean eliminating negative emotions entirely but rather managing them effectively, recognizing and accepting what we feel without being overwhelmed. There are several practical techniques that can help create a stable emotional foundation, allowing us to face daily challenges with greater calm and clarity. Here are some effective methods:

1. **Practicing Meditation** Meditation is an ancient practice that fosters awareness of the present moment. Through meditation, we learn to observe our thoughts and feelings without judgment or impulsive reactions. It helps develop a calmer, more focused mind, reducing anxiety and enhancing our ability to manage stress. Various forms of meditation, such as mindfulness, guided meditation, and breathing exercises, can be beneficial. Even dedicating just 10–15 minutes a day can make a significant difference, providing a break from daily chaos and cultivating an inner sense of calm. Meditation not only soothes the mind but also builds emotional resilience, equipping us to handle difficulties with greater serenity, as previously discussed.

2. **Regular Physical Exercise** Physical activity is one of the most natural and effective ways to improve emotional balance. Exercise releases endorphins, often referred to as the "happy hormones," which boost mood and reduce stress. Regular physical activity, whether it's walking, yoga, running, or any form of exercise you enjoy, not only keeps the body healthy but also helps regulate emotions and maintain a positive outlook.

3. **Reflective Journaling** Journaling is a powerful tool for processing emotions and achieving greater mental clarity. Writing allows us to explore our thoughts and feelings, identify patterns, and gain insights into what troubles us. Keeping a regular reflective journal helps release pent, up emotions, confront fears, and find solutions to problems in a more rational and creative manner. Over time, reviewing our journal entries can show us how much we have grown and how we have overcome difficult situations.

4. **Practicing Gratitude** Gratitude is a simple yet potent practice for improving emotional balance. Taking time each day to reflect on what we are grateful for helps shift our focus from problems to blessings, even during challenging times. Keeping a gratitude journal and noting three things we're thankful for each day can transform our mindset, fostering a more positive outlook. Gratitude not only enhances our mood but also strengthens our capacity to handle stress and encourages a more optimistic view of life.

5. **Learning to Say No** Setting healthy boundaries is crucial for emotional balance. Learning to say no to requests that overwhelm us or do not align with our values and needs allows us to protect our time and energy. Saying no is not selfish; it's a way to care for ourselves and preserve our well-being. Practicing assertiveness and communicating our limits with respect and clarity reduces stress and prevents burnout, contributing to a more balanced and satisfying life, as previously explored.

6. **Cultivating Positive Relationships** Healthy, supportive relationships are vital for emotional balance. Connecting with people who understand, support, and encourage us helps us feel less alone and more understood. It's important to surround ourselves with individuals who respect our boundaries and offer empathetic listening. Dedicating time to nurturing these relationships through meaningful conversations and shared moments reinforces our sense of belonging and provides essential support during challenging times.

7. **Practicing Self, Care** Self, care is not a luxury but a necessity for maintaining emotional balance. This includes engaging in activities that relax and recharge us, such as taking a warm bath, reading, listening to music, or enjoying nature. Self, care also involves getting enough sleep, following a balanced diet, and dedicating time to hobbies and passions that bring joy. Investing in self, care keeps us energetic, motivated, and capable of facing challenges with a serene mind and an open heart.

Emotional balance is a skill that can be cultivated through daily practices and a consistent commitment to personal well, being. Embracing these techniques helps us build a more harmonious life, where our emotions guide us toward greater personal growth and fulfillment, rather than overwhelming us.

Practicing Mindfulness Daily

Mindfulness is a powerful practice that involves paying attention to the present moment without judgment. By focusing on what is happening right now, we can experience a greater sense of calm and clarity. In today's fast, paced world, filled with distractions and stressors, incorporating mindfulness into our daily routines can provide significant emotional and psychological benefits. This practice allows us to step back from automatic responses, bringing awareness to our thoughts, emotions, and physical sensations, and consciously choosing our reactions.

1. Starting with Simple Breathing Exercises

One of the simplest ways to begin practicing mindfulness is through mindful breathing. For 10, 15 minutes a day, find a quiet place where you can sit or lie down comfortably. Close your eyes and take slow, deep breaths, paying close attention to the sensation of air entering and leaving your body. Notice how your chest rises and falls, and how the air feels cool as it enters your nostrils and warm as it exits. This simple act of focusing on your breath helps calm the mind and reduce feelings of stress and anxiety. If your mind starts to wander, gently guide your focus back to your breath without judgment.

2. **Practicing Mindfulness During Daily Activities**

   Mindfulness doesn't require a special setting or a significant time commitment. You can practice it during everyday activities such as eating, walking, or even doing household chores. For example, when eating, pay attention to the taste, texture, and aroma of your food. Notice the colors and shapes on your plate, and savor each bite without distractions like watching TV or checking your phone. Similarly, when walking, feel the ground beneath your feet, notice the rhythm of your steps, and observe your surroundings with fresh eyes. These small actions transform ordinary moments into opportunities for mindfulness, helping you stay connected to the present.

3. **Using Mindfulness to Manage Stress and Emotions**

   Mindfulness is also a valuable tool for managing stress and difficult emotions. When you notice feelings of anxiety, frustration, or sadness, pause and take a moment to observe what you are experiencing. Instead of reacting immediately, acknowledge your feelings and explore them with curiosity. Ask yourself what thoughts are associated with these emotions and where you feel them in your body. By doing so, you create a space between the emotion and your response, allowing for a more measured and thoughtful reaction. This practice helps prevent emotional reactions from overwhelming you and reduces the likelihood of responding in ways you might regret later.

4. Incorporating Mindfulness into Your Morning Routine

Starting your day with mindfulness can set a positive tone for the rest of the day. Try incorporating a short mindfulness practice into your morning routine. This could be as simple as a few minutes of meditation, a mindful stretching session, or even practicing gratitude by acknowledging three things you are thankful for each morning. Beginning the day with intention and awareness helps reduce stress and increases your ability to handle challenges calmly and effectively.

5. Creating a Mindful Space

Designating a specific area in your home for mindfulness practice can encourage you to integrate mindfulness into your daily life. This space doesn't need to be large or elaborately decorated. It could be a corner with a comfortable chair, a soft cushion, or a small altar with items that bring you peace, such as candles, crystals, or plants. Having a designated space serves as a physical reminder to take a moment for yourself, making it easier to practice mindfulness regularly.

6. **Digital Mindfulness**

   In today's technology, driven world, practicing digital mindfulness is also important. This means being aware of how and when you use various devices. Set specific times to check your emails and social media, and create boundaries for screen time. Use your devices consciously, taking breaks to stretch, breathe, and refocus your attention. Digital mindfulness helps reduce the stress associated with constant connectivity and information overload, promoting a healthier relationship with technology.

7. **Mindfulness as a Lifelong Practice**

   Finally, it's important to remember that mindfulness is a continuous practice, not a quick fix. The benefits of mindfulness, such as reduced stress, enhanced emotional resilience, and a greater sense of well, being, build over time. Be patient with yourself as you integrate these practices into your daily life. Mindfulness is about progress, not perfection. The more consistently you practice, the more naturally it will become a part of your everyday routine, leading to a more balanced and fulfilling life.

Incorporating mindfulness into daily life offers a path to greater self, awareness, emotional balance, and a deeper connection to the present moment. By cultivating mindfulness, we learn to navigate life's challenges with greater ease and to find joy and peace in the here and now.

Chapter 14:
Moving Forward with Confidence

As we come to the close of this journey of personal growth and transformation, it's essential to recognize that reaching this point is a significant achievement. Feeling more self, aware, emotionally balanced, and capable of setting healthy boundaries is already a powerful foundation upon which to build a fulfilling life. However, this journey is ongoing, and the lessons you've learned are tools to carry with you as you continue to evolve and face new challenges.

In this final chapter, we'll focus on how to keep your momentum strong, applying what you've learned to your daily life with consistency and intention. Moving forward with confidence doesn't mean you'll never face doubt or fear again, it means having the resilience and tools to navigate those moments with inner strength and clarity.

Embracing Continuous Growth

It's important to remember that personal growth is not a destination but a lifelong journey. There will always be new challenges and opportunities for development. By embracing the mindset of a lifelong learner, you can stay open to new experiences and continue evolving. This means staying curious, being willing to ask questions, and maintaining a humble attitude toward learning from life's ups and downs.

Setting Clear, Realistic Goals

Setting goals is a vital part of moving forward with confidence. These goals should reflect your values and aspirations, offering you direction and purpose. However, it's crucial to set goals that are both challenging and achievable. Using the SMART criteria (Specific, Measurable, Achievable, Relevant, Time, bound) can help you create goals that motivate and inspire you without leading to frustration or burnout.

Developing an Actionable Plan

Having a clear plan of action for how to achieve your goals is equally important. This plan should include:

- **Short, Term Steps:** Identify immediate actions you can take to start moving towards your goals. These steps should be manageable and specific.

- **Long, Term Vision:** Envision where you want to be in the future and the major milestones you need to reach along the way.

- **Flexibility:** Be prepared to adapt your plan as circumstances change. Life is unpredictable, and flexibility allows you to stay on track even when things don't go as expected.

Cultivating a Positive Mindset

Your mindset plays a critical role in how you experience and respond to challenges. Cultivating a positive, growth, oriented mindset helps you see setbacks as opportunities for learning and improvement rather than as failures. Practices such as gratitude, positive affirmations, and mindfulness can help reinforce this mindset, allowing you to approach life with optimism and resilience.

Staying Connected to Your Values

As you move forward, it's essential to stay connected to your core values. These values serve as a compass, guiding your decisions and helping you remain aligned with your true self. Regularly reflecting on your values and how your actions align with them can provide clarity and direction, especially during times of uncertainty or challenge.

Building a Support Network

No one can achieve their goals in isolation. Building and maintaining a strong support network of friends, family, mentors, and like, minded individuals can provide encouragement, guidance, and accountability as you work towards your goals. Don't hesitate to seek support or share your journey with those you trust, they can offer valuable insights and help you stay motivated.

Handling Setbacks with Grace

Setbacks are inevitable, but how you respond to them makes all the difference. When faced with a challenge or failure, take a moment to reflect on what happened, what you can learn from the experience, and how you can move forward. Practicing self, compassion and patience with yourself during these times is crucial for maintaining your confidence and resilience.

Practicing Self, Care

Continuing to prioritize self, care is vital for maintaining the energy and focus needed to pursue your goals. Regularly engaging in activities that nurture your mind, body, and spirit helps you stay balanced and grounded. This might include exercise, meditation, creative pursuits, or simply taking time to relax and recharge.

Celebrating Your Progress

Take time to acknowledge and celebrate your achievements, no matter how small they may seem. Recognizing your progress helps reinforce positive behaviors and keeps you motivated. Celebrate your successes, reflect on your growth, and use these moments as fuel to keep moving forward.

Creating a Vision for the Future

Finally, as you move forward with confidence, it's helpful to have a clear vision of what you want your future to look like. This vision should reflect not only your goals but also the kind of person you want to become. Take some time to imagine your ideal life, considering all aspects, career, relationships, health, personal fulfillment, and let this vision inspire and guide your daily actions.

Final Thoughts

Moving forward with confidence is about embracing the journey of life with courage, curiosity, and commitment to your growth. By continuing to apply the principles and practices you've learned, you can navigate life's challenges with resilience and grace, creating a life that is truly aligned with your highest aspirations.

Are you ready to take this next step with courage and confidence? Let's move forward, embracing each moment and every opportunity for growth with an open heart and a strong, determined spirit.

Embracing New Beginnings

Embracing a new beginning means acknowledging that each phase of life presents an opportunity to renew, learn, and grow. Change can be intimidating, especially when it pushes us out of our comfort zone, but it's often during these moments that we develop new skills and strengthen our resilience. A new beginning is not merely the end of one chapter or a transition; it's an open door to countless possibilities. Let's delve deeper into what it means to embrace new beginnings and explore practical and emotional aspects to navigate this process with confidence.

1. **Recognizing Its Importance**

   Change, whether chosen or unexpected, is often essential for personal growth. Without it, we remain stagnant. Each new beginning is an opportunity to reflect on your life, take a step forward, and leave behind what no longer serves you. This might mean re, evaluating relationships, career paths, or daily habits. Consider making a list of situations or habits you'd like to change and reflect on how these shifts can support your personal development.

2. **Letting Go of Past Expectations**

   Letting go is an act of liberation. Often, we cling to what's familiar out of fear of the unknown, even when it no longer fulfills us. Embracing new beginnings means understanding that the past does not define who you are today. Releasing old expectations, disappointments, or failures allows you to move forward unburdened, making room for new opportunities. Working on forgiveness, both towards others and yourself, is key. Giving yourself permission to have made mistakes in the past is an important step towards fully embracing the future. Remember that each life path is unique, and the lessons learned from things not going as planned are invaluable.

3. Developing a Growth Mindset

Adopting a growth mindset is essential for successfully embracing new beginnings. This concept, developed by psychologist Carol Dweck, involves believing that abilities and intelligence can be developed through effort and perseverance. With a growth mindset, challenges are viewed not as obstacles but as opportunities to grow. Changing your inner dialogue is an effective way to cultivate this mindset. Instead of saying, "I can't do this, " try thinking, "I can't do this yet, but I can learn." Every new challenge is an opportunity to acquire new skills and improve yourself.

4. Embracing Uncertainty

One of the most challenging aspects of new beginnings is the uncertainty that often accompanies them. It's natural to want to know exactly what will happen, but much of life is unpredictable. Embracing uncertainty means accepting that while you cannot control every event, you can control your attitude towards them. This doesn't mean giving up on planning but rather recognizing that some elements will always be unpredictable. Practices like meditation and mindfulness can help develop a greater tolerance for uncertainty, teaching you to stay present and navigate challenges with more mental flexibility.

5. **Building a Vision for the Future**

   Having a clear vision for the future is crucial for moving forward with confidence. This vision doesn't need to be rigid but should serve as a general guide that inspires you to work towards what you truly want. Writing down your goals, dividing them into short, medium, and long, term milestones, can be very helpful. These goals should be realistic yet challenging enough to promote growth. Review them regularly, adjust as necessary, and celebrate the small successes along the way.

6. **Accepting the Emotions That Come with Change**

   Every change comes with emotional weight. It's normal to feel a mix of excitement and fear when starting something new. Rather than suppress these emotions, it's important to acknowledge and accept them. Being in tune with your feelings, without letting them take over, helps you process them healthily and move forward without being stuck. Practicing self, compassion is essential. Accept that there will be days when you feel discouraged, and that's okay. Treat yourself with the kindness and understanding you would offer a friend in a similar situation. Allowing space for these emotions enables you to process them and move forward more effectively.

7. **Building a Support Network**

   Although change is often a personal challenge, having a supportive community can make a significant difference. Sharing your new beginnings with trusted individuals who encourage and support you helps maintain motivation and overcome difficult times. Create a support network of people who share your values and are ready to cheer you on. This can include friends, family, mentors, or support groups. Being part of a community that believes in your potential provides strength during moments of doubt.

Embracing new beginnings requires courage, patience, and a commitment to ongoing personal growth. Each new challenge is an opportunity to reinvent yourself and build a more authentic and fulfilling life. By maintaining an open mindset, developing emotional resilience, and surrounding yourself with positive support, you can approach the future with greater confidence and optimism.

Setting Future Goals

Setting goals is crucial for maintaining progress and motivation in your personal growth journey. Goals not only provide direction but also serve as a framework to unlock your potential. Without a clear vision of where you want to go, it's easy to feel lost or stagnant. This process isn't just about setting targets but defining goals that align with your values and inspire growth.

Defining Specific and Realistic Goals

A common mistake when setting goals is being too vague. Effective goals need to be specific and measurable. For example, instead of saying, "I want to improve my career," a more refined version would be, "I want to acquire a new technical skill over the next six months through a specific course." Goals should be realistic, ambitious yet achievable, to avoid frustration and demotivation. A well, defined goal allows you to track progress and make adjustments as needed.

Using the SMART Method

The SMART method is a powerful tool for creating clear and achievable goals. It stands for:

- **Specific:** Clearly define what you want to achieve.

- **Measurable:** Determine how you will measure progress or success.

- **Attainable:** Ensure the goal is achievable with your available resources.

- **Relevant:** Align the goal with your values and priorities.

- **Time, bound:** Set a realistic deadline for achieving the goal.

Using this structure ensures that your goals are concrete and actionable.

Breaking Goals into Short, Medium, and Long, Term Milestones

Divide your goals into smaller, manageable milestones. Setting only large, long, term goals can feel overwhelming. Create an action plan that includes:

- **Short, term goals:** Actions you can take in the next few weeks.

- **Medium, term goals:** Steps to take in the coming months.

- **Long, term goals:** Achievements to aim for over a year or more.

This approach helps maintain motivation by allowing you to celebrate intermediate successes on the path to your final goal.

Adapting to Changes

Remember that goals should be flexible. Life changes, and what once seemed important may no longer be relevant. Adjusting your goals as your priorities or circumstances shift doesn't mean abandoning them but adapting to remain aligned with your personal evolution.

Monitoring and Reevaluating Progress

Regularly monitor your progress. Keeping track of your actions and challenges helps you reflect on what's working and what could be improved. Reviewing your goals monthly or quarterly allows you to assess your progress and make necessary adjustments.

Celebrating Successes

Celebrate your successes, both big and small. Recognizing and celebrating progress keeps you motivated and helps maintain a positive mindset. Celebrations don't need to be elaborate; a simple reward or acknowledgment is enough to reinforce your progress and commitment.

In summary, setting future goals gives you a clear vision and guides your life in alignment with your deepest desires and values. Each goal, no matter how small, contributes to building a meaningful and fulfilling life. Stay flexible, open to change, and regularly assess your progress to make achieving your goals a natural part of your journey.

Guided Visualization: Your Ideal Future

Guided visualization is a powerful technique for connecting with your vision of the future and clarifying your goals. This exercise helps you imagine your "ideal self" in detail, aligning your daily actions to achieve that vision. Visualization can reinforce your belief in your goals and strengthen your commitment to achieving them.

1. **Create a Comfortable Space** Before you begin, find a quiet place where you won't be disturbed for at least 15, 20 minutes. Make sure you feel comfortable and relaxed, whether you choose to sit, lie down, or use a cushion, whatever helps you feel centered and at ease.

2. **Begin with Mindful Breathing** Start by focusing on your breath to calm your mind and bring yourself into the present moment. Breathe in slowly through your nose for a count of four, hold for two seconds, then exhale gently for a count of six. Repeat this cycle for a few minutes, allowing each breath to relax you further and help you focus.

3. **Visualize Your Future Self** Project yourself into the future. Choose a time frame that feels right, whether it's one year, five years, or even ten. Begin to build a clear and detailed image of your ideal self. Imagine a "movie" where you are both the director and the main character.

- **Where are you?** Picture your surroundings. Are you in a different home, an office, or a natural environment? Pay attention to the details: the colors, sounds, and light around you.

- **How do you feel?** Focus on the emotions associated with this future. Are you happy, satisfied, and at peace? Feel these positive emotions and let them envelop you.

- **Who is with you?** Visualize the people around you. Are they family, friends, or colleagues? What are your relationships like with them? How do you interact with others in your ideal future?

- **What are you doing?** Imagine yourself engaged in fulfilling activities. Are you working in a career you love, pursuing hobbies, or enjoying relaxation? What brings you joy and satisfaction?

4. **Deepen Your Vision** Don't just focus on the external aspects, connect with the physical and emotional sensations of your future self. How does your body feel? Is your mind clear and calm? This level of detail strengthens your connection to your vision, making it feel more tangible and attainable.

5. **Facing Challenges** Consider a challenge you might encounter in your ideal future. Visualize yourself handling this situation with calm and confidence. Imagine overcoming the difficulty with resilience and emotional intelligence, learning and growing from the experience. This prepares you to see obstacles as opportunities rather than setbacks.

6. **Integrate the Vision into Your Present Life** Now that you've visualized your ideal future, think about what you can start doing today to move closer to that vision. Is there a skill you want to develop, a relationship to nurture, or a habit you want to change? Identify specific actions you can take to begin aligning your present with your ideal future.

7. **Closure and Gratitude** Before ending the visualization, take a moment to thank yourself for committing time to this practice. Feel gratitude for the clarity and determination you've cultivated. Picture your current self moving confidently toward your ideal future, knowing that every step you take brings you closer to your goals.

8. **Daily Practice** Consistency is key. Dedicate a few minutes each day to visualizing your ideal future and reconnecting with the positive feelings it evokes. This will reinforce your commitment and help you stay focused on your goals, even when challenges arise.

This guided visualization exercise helps you align your thoughts and actions with your aspirations, fostering a mindset of growth and success. By regularly practicing and visualizing your future, you cultivate a strong sense of purpose and direction, empowering you to create the life you envision.

Websites and Communities for Emotional Support

When it comes to emotional healing and personal growth, finding the right support can make a significant difference. In addition to personal reflection and the practices discussed earlier, having access to online communities and reliable resources provides a sense of belonging and guidance. These websites and platforms offer practical advice, peer support, and expert insights, helping individuals navigate their emotional challenges. In this section, you'll find a curated selection of websites and communities specifically designed to provide emotional support, guiding you on your journey toward mental well, being. Whether you're looking for professional counseling, mindfulness tools, or simply a safe space to share your experiences, these resources are here to support you.

Blog: Tiny Buddha

- **Website**: www.tinybuddha.com

Tiny Buddha offers personal stories, mindfulness tips, and advice on personal growth. It covers a broad range of topics, such as emotional resilience, healing from trauma, self, love, and creating healthy relationships, making it perfect for readers who need regular, heartfelt, and practical advice.

Website: PositivePsychology.com

- **Website**: www.positivepsychology.com

PositivePsychology.com provides science, based resources on emotional well, being, personal development, and mental health. The site includes practical exercises, tools, and in, depth articles on various emotional and psychological topics, helping individuals enhance their emotional intelligence and mindfulness.

Instagram: @mindbodygreen

- **Instagram handle**: @mindbodygreen

MindBodyGreen focuses on wellness, emotional health, and personal growth through a holistic approach. The account shares bite, sized insights, inspirational quotes, and expert advice on topics like mindfulness, mental health, and balanced living, ideal for the Instagram generation seeking personal growth and well, being.

YouTube: Lavendaire

- **YouTube Channel**: Lavendaire

Aileen Xu's "Lavendaire" channel focuses on personal development, self, care, and creating a life you love. Her content includes practical tips on productivity, overcoming challenges, self, discovery, and emotional healing, which align perfectly with your target audience's needs.

Final Words from the Author

As I sit here reflecting on the journey we've taken together through this book, I'm filled with gratitude. Writing these pages has been more than sharing tools and strategies; it has been a heartfelt way to connect with you, with the hope of offering support and encouragement. I've shared parts of my own life, my struggles and triumphs, in the hope that you, too, can find your unique path toward healing and growth.

I know that change is challenging. It demands patience, courage, and a willingness to face the unknown. But there is beauty in this process. Every step, no matter how small, brings you closer to who you truly are. Each time you overcome an obstacle, set a boundary, or practice mindfulness, you are building a life that reflects your true self and your deepest values.

I hope you leave this book with a strong belief in your ability to grow, heal, and create a life that fills you with peace, fulfillment, and joy. By choosing to seek knowledge and tools for understanding yourself, you've already taken the most courageous step. Now, it's about moving forward with confidence and compassion.

Remember, challenges will arise, and that's part of the journey. Growth isn't a straight line, and it's during those tough times that you will discover your greatest strengths. Trust yourself, be gentle with yourself, and know that every effort you make is bringing you closer to your most authentic self.

Thank you for allowing me to be a part of your journey. My wish for you is that you continue moving forward with an open heart, embracing every new beginning, and always believing in the incredible power within you.

With Love And Gratitude,
Carina Marvel

If in any way this book was helpful to you, I would be infinitely grateful if you would leave me an honest review by scanning the following qr code: Thank you from the bottom of my heart.

Manufactured by Amazon.ca
Acheson, AB

14542392R00136